DUNMORE

D1403786

John IV Earl of Dunmore.
Courtesy of the Scottish National Gallery, Edinburgh.

DUNMORE

by John E. Selby

Edward M. Riley, *Editor*

Published by the

Virginia Independence Bicentennial Commission

Box JF

Williamsburg, Virginia 23185

v

DUNMORE

In the dark of early morning Thursday, June 8, 1775, a group of figures stole through the grounds of the Governor's Palace in Williamsburg, Virginia, furtively winding their way out of the city. At their head was the royal governor, Lord Dunmore, and with him were his wife Charlotte and their children, three boys and four girls ranging in age from fifteen years to six months. The governor's aide, Capt. Edward Foy, and Mrs. Foy and several servants accompanied them. Although armed volunteers were on watch in town and there must have been noise with the children and their baggage, the group escaped unobserved and by the next day reached Yorktown. There they boarded H.M.S. *Fowey*.

Dunmore was afraid for his life or that he and his family might be seized as hostages. For ten years American colonists had been quarreling with Great Britain over Parliament's right to tax them, and Dunmore's efforts in recent months to still opposition to British measures had focused the animosities of the previous decade squarely upon him. A few weeks before, Thomas Jefferson considered him to be "in the last danger" from an aroused populace. Even then, the venerable statesman of the Virginia legislature, Richard Bland, was talking of hanging him.

Consternation swept through the town at the news of his successful flight. The simultaneous arrival of the sloop H.M.S. *Otter* in the York River made it seem that he had word of an approaching invasion; a short while later, reports that Gov. Josiah Martin of North Carolina had fled from his capital at New Bern just a few days before Dunmore's escape appeared to confirm that supposition. "Lord Dunmore and governor Martin have certainly compared notes," remarked the editor of the *Virginia Gazette* on printing the news.

Denunciations of Dunmore arose on every side. Of all the governors in the last years of British rule, only Thomas Hutchinson of Massachusetts could contend with him for the title of most despised.

For the next fourteen months Dunmore plagued Virginians. He raided their coasts and seized their ships and, by offering freedom to any of their slaves who would fight against them, threatened to give bloody reality to the nightmares that slaveholders have. The anger that he aroused goaded Virginians to seek independence from Great Britain, although they probably would have done so anyway. He mainly provided a real-life example of the tyranny that they came to see in British rule. He could have become dangerous. There was always the chance that an invasion fleet might appear in Chesapeake Bay; one did head in Virginia's direction but turned away for South Carolina. But never in close communication with the British high command, Dunmore was not a major figure in its strategy. He received few reinforcements, and despite his boasts, inspired few loyalists, either black or white, to join him. Those whom he did command he wasted in hopeless tactics.

Yet just six months before his flight Dunmore had returned to Williamsburg a conquering hero after leading a successful expedition at considerable risk and hardship to himself against the Indians of the Ohio Valley in the first Dunmore's War. As a result, he could only ascribe his current difficulties to the grossest ingratitude. "I have once fought for Virginians," he swore, "and, by God, I will let them see that I can fight against them." Nor did he anticipate great opposition. His popularity as an Indian fighter convinced him that most Virginians were on his side. All that was needed, he persistently told the British government, was a small show of force by the crown, an indication that it would protect its supporters and teach the rebels a lesson, and he was confident that he would soon have the bulk of the population behind him. Almost as incredibly, the ministry believed him.

It was this assessment that kept Dunmore from understanding the depth of the unrest he confronted. It led him repeatedly to take risks to suppress Virginians that made him seem either a fool or, more likely, a would-be oppressor with an armada bearing down on the coast. Virginians could not believe that he did not know how extensive the opposition to British policy really was. He would hardly have dared to taunt them as he did with the few forces at his command unless others were on the way.

Dunmore seemed actually to want war. The eventual outcome

notwithstanding, at the time of his flight most Virginians had no desire to leave the British empire, despite their determination to defend their liberty. They were not unhappy to be Englishmen. One of their dearest beliefs was that it was only because they were that they had liberties to defend. No other people since ancient times had enjoyed such freedom. Despite years of constitutional wrangling with the mother country, their animosity was not directed toward Englishmen in general, only those who seemed to be perversely working against accommodation—like the governor. He said that he fled for his life, but the House of Burgesses pointed out that he had walked across town alone to visit the attorney general, John Randolph, the evening before he left. The implication was that he was seizing upon the threats of a few hotheads for his own purpose.

To prove their point the burgesses took careful testimony, some from British merchants unfortunate enough to be in Williamsburg, to substantiate a long resolution recounting the events of the last few months, alleging that it was Dunmore who had started all the trouble. However arguable their version, a substantial majority of the assembly obviously did not want a break with the mother country and were provoked at Dunmore for persisting in an account that could precipitate it. He must have an ulterior motive. Why else would he say that they were rebels when they so wanted to be loyal?

The truth was that most British had become convinced that a firm hand was needed in the colonies long before Virginians and most other Americans were aware of their attitude. At the same time, the British did not see themselves as deliberately trying to oppress America. To the contrary, most of them were as proud as Americans of the vaunted freedom of Englishmen, which included colonists. Few in Parliament had direct interests in America; most thought of the colonies only when they had to. But when they did, with hardly an exception, they were quite clear as to whose empire it was and were all too ready to rebuke any who might seem to have forgotten. The strongest element in their reaction to American resistance was outraged national pride. The result was that, as more and more of them began to reflect this feeling, their remarks and activities, many of which were entirely independent of each other, took on a conspiratorial character in the minds of Americans.

Dunmore's actions, for example, were for the most part impulsively his own and were not coordinated with Gov. Martin or anyone else. In fact, there was ridiculously little communication between him and his superiors for so critical a time. For a long while he paid little attention to imperial affairs but concentrated on local and personal matters. During the year following the Boston Tea Party in December 1773, when ministerial policy was hardening, he almost totally neglected his responsibilities to London. Yet he was completely attuned to the decision to force a showdown in America when it came. After that, it was not his nature to dawdle once duty and interest were clear. A hearty, athletic man, he had a vigorous, red-blooded point of view and a penchant for action rather than words—qualities that help explain his earlier success among men of a similar cast in subduing what was then the American West. Most likely, his superiors would have preferred that he waited, for they were involved in Massachusetts and were not prepared to deal with more than one colony at a time. On the other hand, when they did communicate with him, it is clear that they welcomed success if he could achieve it on his own. Fundamentally there was no difference between his attitude and London's. It was his kind of people who then ruled the British empire, and as Virginians came to realize this they turned to independence. Had they known earlier, they might have been ready long before.

I

JOHN MURRAY, fourth earl of Dunmore, Viscount Fincastle, baron of Blair, Moulin, and Tillemot, was one of the many Scots in the eighteenth century who abandoned old hatreds of England to take advantage of the Act of Union of 1707 to enter wholeheartedly into British life. A relatively poor country at the beginning of the century, Scotland benefited enormously from the union, and at the same time returned to England as much as it took through the contributions of its people to the British Enlightenment and the great economic resurgence of the period. Scots were everywhere: in commerce, banking, and industry, in the military and imperial services, in the church, in science, in arts and letters, and at court. Inevitably there was a reaction. Despite, or perhaps because of, their success, Scots were not liked by eighteenth-century Englishmen, who remained particularly suspicious of their political principles.

One of the suppositions Virginians had about Dunmore was that he was just showing his colors in the American Revolution since his family had always been tories and supporters of the old House of Stuart, whose name was synonymous with tyranny in English history books of the day. Actually, in contemporary political parlance, Dunmore was a whig—that is, he accepted the Glorious Revolution of 1688 which established the supremacy of Parliament, and he endorsed the accession of the House of Hanover in 1714 to the British throne. True, some of his ancestors had backed the rival claims of the Scottish Stuarts, but more had accepted the inevitable and joined the English establishment. Because in the seventeenth century the Stuart king, James II, had created Dunmore's great uncle, Charles Murray, the first earl, the latter had remained loyal to that monarch during the Glorious Revolution, and under James's successors, William and

5

Mary, had been arrested on suspicion several times. But under Queen Anne, whom he had served as master of horse when she was a young princess, the first earl returned to favor and espoused the Act of Union.

The second earl, Charles Murray's son, pursued the same policy under the Hanoverians. He became a lord of the bedchamber to King George II and one of his principal generals, high in command at the battle of Dettingen in 1743. To the general's embarrassment, however, his brother William, who had married into a proscribed Jacobite family, the Nairnes, enlisted under the Stuart pretender, Charles Edward, in the uprising of 1745. Only the general's "great interest" at court won commutation of William's sentence from execution to house arrest for life and enabled him to inherit the title in 1752 when his bachelor brother died.

Four years later the title passed to William's son, John, the future governor of Virginia, who already had chosen to follow his uncle's career rather than his father's. He was then twenty-six years old (or possibly twenty-four—the records vary) and had been serving in the 3rd Foot Guards—his uncle's old regiment—for seven years. The army introduced him to the courtly social life of Europe during tours of duty on the Continent and to an intimate circle of young officers that included James Wolfe, later the conqueror of Quebec; Lord Howe and Baron Cathcart, both of whom subsequently fought in America; Lord George Lennox, brother of the duke of Richmond; and especially Lord Fitzmaurice, the future earl of Shelburne, with whom he formed a particularly close attachment.

Early in 1758, during the Seven Years' War with France, King George II refused Dunmore permission to serve under the Brunswick commander, Prince Ferdinand, where in the eyes of young officers romance and glory were to be found. Instead, George remarked, if Dunmore wanted to show his courage he should go to the Indies. To Dunmore's chagrin he was ordered to Canada just as Wolfe's campaign against Quebec was commencing, although in the end he somehow avoided the assignment. The reasons for the episode are not clear, although they seem more related to the king's pique at growing criticism of his war policy by younger officers than to Dunmore personally. At any rate, Dunmore was not with Fitzmaurice and the rest of the 3rd Regiment at the battles of Minden and Kloster Kampen, where Fitzmaurice's heroism led to his appointment as aide-de-camp to the king.

In February 1759 Dunmore married Charlotte, the beautiful daughter of the earl of Galloway, and the next year resigned his commission to enter politics. Perhaps the reason was his marriage, or possibly that he had not won preferment as rapidly as his friends—he was still only a captain—for he seems not to have been averse to military life and through Fitzmaurice continued to seek a suitable post to which he could be reinstated.

About the time of Dunmore's resignation, Fitzmaurice informed him that it had been arranged for him to be chosen one of the sixteen representative peers that under the Act of Union Scottish nobles were entitled to elect to the English House of Lords. Dunmore's uncle, the general, had held a similar position from 1727 until his death, as now Dunmore would, except when he was in Virginia, until 1790. During this period, election to these positions was largely in the control of the government, primarily through the offices of the duke of Argyll, who managed Scottish politics for the ministry.

About this time a transition was occurring that was accelerated by the accession of George III in the fall of 1760. The earl of Bute was emerging as the new monarch's favorite and was being groomed to succeed Argyll, as he did upon the duke's death the next year. Intricate ministerial negotiations were taking place, in which Fitzmaurice's father was deeply involved—quite likely an important factor in Dunmore's advancement. Then, when his friend's father suddenly died in the spring of 1761, Dunmore's prospects soared as Fitzmaurice inherited not only his father's title and estates as earl of Shelburne, but also his role as a political lieutenant of Lord Bute.

For the next ten years Dunmore tried hard to break into the upper echelons of British politics. He took up residence in London for the annual social season that accompanied parliamentary sessions and was diligent in attending the House of Lords, although not active in its debates. In 1764, on the death of the duke of Atholl, a senior of the Murray clan, he considered supporting his brother for a seat in the House of Commons from Perthshire, which the duke had controlled. To have seats in Commons dependent upon one was a major bargaining point in eighteenth-century politics. But Shelburne warned him off for fear of antagonizing Atholl's heir.

Shelburne was Dunmore's principal hope during these years, but since he was himself out of office for many of them, there was little he could do. Another reason was that Dunmore insisted upon obtaining a place that would not require him to abandon his political base in the

House of Lords. Finally in 1766, Shelburne returned to office in the second administration of William Pitt, now earl of Chatham, and Dunmore apparently expected a significant appointment but to no avail. At this point the existing correspondence with Shelburne abruptly ends, although whether because of historical accident or a falling out cannot be told. The final letters certainly are as friendly as ever. More likely, Dunmore sought a more promising patron, since Shelburne was acquiring a reputation for political inconsistency that limited his own political future.

Ever since Dunmore had entered the House of Lords he had also cultivated the followers of the duke of Bedford, known as "the Bloomsbury Gang." Shelburne had joined them as they gathered around Lord Bute in the first years of George III's reign under the umbrella of a common conviction that the Seven Years' War had to end. Despite Britain's overwhelming success against the French in almost every part of the empire, by the time Dunmore entered Parliament there was growing sentiment that the astronomical cost outweighed any advantage in pursuing further victories.

One of Dunmore's few recorded political stands was an outraged protest in conjunction with Bedford and a Shelburnite against a bill for continuing the war. Later, Dunmore asked Lord Weymouth, one of Bedford's chief associates, to be godfather of his second son. The alliance was cemented in 1768 when another of Bedford's lieutenants, Earl Gower, married Susanna, daughter of the earl of Galloway and Lady Dunmore's older sister. A few months earlier the Bedfordites had entered the ministry—fortuitously for Dunmore since Chatham and Shelburne shortly dropped out. Soon Dunmore again joined Bedford to protest in the House of Lords against an adverse judicial decision in a cause that Bedford had befriended. By then Dunmore seems also to have accepted the fact that his best chance for advancement was overseas, and within a year, in January 1770, the king signed his commission as governor of New York.

Dunmore's motive in going to America was largely financial. This is not to say that he was a penniless noble seeking to recoup his fortune; he was not. His estates in Scotland returned an income of over £3,000 a year. His home was a fine manor house, Dunmore Park, overlooking the Firth of Forth, near Airth, Stirlingshire, around which he owned about 4,000 acres reputed to be among the finest in the British isles. He also had his father's old home, Taymount in Perthshire, and a producing colliery at Ardentenny in Argyllshire.

He maintained a town house in London and freely entertained military and political friends whenever they traveled in Scotland.

While infrequently his papers refer to a tightness of money, there is no sign of serious indebtedness. But in comparison to the men of great fortunes who ran eighteenth-century England, Dunmore was poor; his income was not a tenth that of his friend Shelburne, one of the richest men in the country. Possibly he might have made do, since he did survive in London society for a decade without a significant increment. But there was an ever increasing family, ultimately totaling five sons and four daughters. He frankly admitted that the lure of America was to enhance the patrimony of his children.

What Dunmore's views on America were at this point is uncertain. From the time the Bedfordites entered the cabinet, they tended to urge an increasingly hard line toward the colonies. But it appears unlikely that constitutional issues were burning concerns with Dunmore. He was present in the House of Lords in 1766 during the debate over the repeal of the Stamp Act, for example, and did not join Bedford and Earl Gower in their protest that repeal would render British authority contemptible.

In January 1770, while awaiting his commission, Dunmore did his duty by seconding the congratulatory reply to the king's speech on subjects involving America—that is, he supported the ministry's anti-American position. But in his speech he was reported to have remarked that "the Americans would soon be quiet, if they were only left to themselves." By then, he had clearly separated himself from Shelburne, who with Chatham was now in full opposition to the government's colonial policy. Most likely Dunmore's views on policy at this stage were conditioned less by principle than by his search for office and the need to avoid antagonizing those in power.

II

Dunmore tried to do a good job in America because he intended to establish at least some of his family there permanently. Hardly one to be called a democrat, he nonetheless endeavored to be as popular as he could, for that served to advance his interests. When informed that newly appointed governors customarily called elections for the assembly upon their arrival, he expressed to the ministers his disapproval of the practice, but added, "however I was told, that it would be pleasing to the people, who are no doubt fond of the exercise of that power, which makes them feel their own consequence." He made no secret that he was fortune-hunting, but then so were George Washington and the others who joined him in speculating in western lands. Within these terms he was relatively successful during his early years in office. He was well on his way to his fortune, and while inevitably he made enemies, he was reasonably popular. Had it not been for the American Revolution, he would probably have gone down as a typical mid-eighteenth-century governor of little note in history.

Ignoring the secretary of state's injunction to assume his post as quickly as possible, Dunmore suited his own convenience in departing for New York—an attitude toward his duties that he frequently displayed throughout his public service. Just before his appointment, he and Lady Dunmore were in Paris as guests of the duke of Richmond, father of his old friend Lord George Lennox. Dunmore returned to London for the parliamentary session, but his wife remained abroad until spring. The long-range plan was for her and the children to wait until he determined whether the climate and living conditions in America were suitable for them to follow. By the time she returned from the Continent, and he had settled the family again in Britain and leisurely concluded his personal affairs, it was late summer before he set sail for the colonies.

The delay embroiled him as soon as he landed in New York in October 1770 in a bitter and protracted controversy with the lieutenant governor, Cadwallader Colden, over whether he was entitled to share the fees of office during the period in which Colden did all the work. At the same time Dunmore quickly made friends with another power in New York politics, Sir William Johnson, superintendent of Indian affairs in the northern provinces, and with speculators fighting a battle with New Hampshire interests over lands in the area of modern Vermont, which both New York and New Hampshire then claimed. Dunmore's role as the colony's champion in that controversy insured amicable relations with the New York assembly and afforded as well an opportunity to carve out an estate of some 51,000 acres on Otter Creek, on the shore of Lake Champlain. Justly pleased with his success, Dunmore was dismayed when he was abruptly ordered to Virginia after only a few months at his new post.

The transfer had been arranged by Earl Gower as a promotion, for Virginia was a more populous and wealthier colony than New York. But Dunmore let it be known—to the ministry, to Gower, and to all of New York—that he did not want to go. It would ruin his plans, he wrote his brother-in-law, for not only would he lose a year's success in New York, but his family could never endure the "fevers" of the warmer South. Again he took his time following orders until his successor, William Tryon, actually moved in on him. Then he vacationed for a month on Sir William Johnson's baronial frontier manor before finally departing. An additional stopover in Philadelphia delayed his arrival in Williamsburg until September 25, 1771, well after his opinion of Virginia had preceded him.

Later, Virginians formed the idea that Dunmore had the mark of a tyrant from the beginning: intemperate, arrogant, and lecherous as well. After it was safe to talk about him there were stories of amorous affairs, and he gave evidence of a lack of self-control that hurt his own cause as much as his opponents'. Everyone marveled, too, at the forty-two pipes of wine and twelve gross of bottled liqueurs found in the Palace cellar. But the inference depended upon one's point of view; drinking was hardly a novelty in colonial Virginia. "No Man kept a better House," remarked one observer.

The comparison was usually to Dunmore's immediate predecessor, Lord Botetourt, who in the amazingly short space of two years in office before his sudden death in 1769, had become "beloved" by the people. The House of Burgesses erected a marble statue in the Capitol in his honor. Botetourt's political talents and personal charm, his education and cultural refinement, were outstanding, although any inference that he would have taken the part of the colonists if the imperial crisis had arisen in his administration is dubious. He came from the same circle in Great Britain as Dunmore.

Botetourt's polish, moreover, does not mean that his successor was a boor. Dunmore was as educated and socially accomplished as the average British nobleman of the time, and before imperial affairs intervened, many Virginians found him quite acceptable to their taste. His 1,300-volume library was among the largest in the colonies, and his furnishings for the Palace included three organs, a harpsichord, and a piano. He had an excellent art collection by colonial standards, and was a frequent theatergoer.

The real difference was in disposition. Dunmore, St. George Tucker of Williamsburg once remarked, "was not a man of parade; his predecessor I believe was." Botetourt was a courtly politician. The fact that he was the first noble to reside in the colony as governor in nearly a century flattered Virginians, and he knew how to extract the most from the role. He brought over, for example, a magnificent carriage with a matched team of horses which he had received from the king's uncle, the duke of Cumberland, captain-general of the British army. Riding in the formal attire of his office to the Capitol to convene the assembly, he must have presented a royal appearance. Dunmore, although a noble, was more a robust man of action, who besides his musical instruments and art had a collection of armaments worth one-third of all the furnishings of the Palace, according to one estimate. For dinner and the theater, he favored Virginians who combined drawingroom manners with talk of adventure and the outdoors, like Col. George Washington.

As in New York, Dunmore made enemies in Virginia. He early offended Theodorick Bland in a court case and tried to take the appointment of clerks of the county courts away from the secretary of the colony, Thomas Nelson, until his superiors in London advised him that it was impolitic. He raised a furor when he appointed his aide, Capt. Foy, acting deputy auditor upon the death of the incumbent, John Blair, and increased the fees connected with the office without consulting the legislature. But he apologized that he did not know the assembly had to approve the changes and wined and dined the burgesses to make amends. They reciprocated with a ball in his honor and named a town and county after him during the session. William Nelson, president of the Council and acting governor before Dunmore came, who at first had been irritated by reports of the new governor's comments about Virginia, observed after they had met, "I think I discover many Good Qualities in him."

Still, Dunmore did not forget his background and station in dealings with colonists. He was in the habit of dismissing the legislature, even when they parted amicably, with a little homily. Once he told the members "to infuse that Spirit of Industry, which alone can make a Country flourish, and to promote a strict Observance of that Order and Regularity, which are equally necessary to the Security of all good Government, as well as to the real Welfare of the People." Another time, he advised them to try "to abolish that Spirit of Gaming, which I am afraid but too generally prevails among the People, and to substitute in its place a love of Agriculture, and attention to their private Affairs." He returned to this theme later when events put more bite in his words and frequently told British correspondents that Virginians were basically lazy.

This attitude of paternalism toward colonists may explain the abrupt change of mood that could occur whenever Dunmore felt that his good intentions were unappreciated. His first real quarrel with the legislature came in 1773 over a counterfeiting case in Pittsylvania County, which arose when the assembly was not in session. Dunmore carefully consulted the treasurer, the speaker of the House of Burgesses, and members of the Council, all of whom advised sending the militia to arrest the culprits and calling the assembly to avoid a financial crisis. The militia, however, brought their prisoners directly to Williamsburg to be bound over to the General Court, and although the courts subsequently upheld the procedure, the burgesses criticized the governor for endangering "the safety of innocent Men" by not holding a hearing in Pittsylvania first as was more customary. Dunmore was enraged and retorted that he had acted in good faith. Subject to the determination of the courts, he said, "I shall continue to exercise the Powers I am invested with, whensoever the exigencies of Government, and the good of the Country requires such exertion" and "no one (even the most timid)" need fear for the innocent as a consequence.

But for several years the overriding concern in Virginia was the opening of the West, an issue on which Dunmore's aggressiveness fitted Virginian predilections perfectly. After the emotions of the American Revolution, some charged that the governor had used the West to distract Virginians from the quarrel with Great Britain. There were allegations that he tried to sow disunity by stirring up a dispute with Pennsylvania over title to the area around Fort Pitt (modern Pittsburgh); that he exaggerated the danger of Indian attack to exhaust the western militia in frontier skirmishes, or perhaps to raise a western army to fight revolutionaries in the East. Actually, if anyone suffered from Dunmore's western policy, it was the British. He did virtually nothing that he was instructed to do with regard to the West, and nothing else seemed to occupy his attention at a most crucial moment in imperial history.

More than in New York, Dunmore found the issue of opening new lands to settlement a perfect means of combining his ambition for profit and popularity. Land was the road to wealth in Virginia; almost everyone of consequence was concerned. George Washington in particular became a frequent guest at the Governor's Palace and a companion at the theater, for apart from his own personal investment, he represented veterans who had bounty claims from the French and Indian War. In the summer of 1773, Washington was to go with Dunmore to introduce him to the West, but family affairs at the last moment interfered and the governor pushed on alone. In the process of acquainting himself with the colony's problems in the West on this trip, Dunmore put in a claim for 20,000 acres for each of his five sons, plus 10,000 for his aide, Capt. Foy.

Dunmore's instructions contained numerous restrictions in line with British policy over the preceding decade inhibiting settlement beyond the Appalachian Mountains. For reasons of economy in defense, concern over colonial treatment of the Indians, and a worry that Britain could not effectively administer territory so far from the sea, the ministry had issued a proclamation in 1763, at the end of the French and Indian War, excluding colonists from the vast area just wrested from France. Subsequent negotiations had produced relatively little modification in the policy. But now there were reports that the Walpole Company of Philadelphia, which numbered several cabinet ministers among its backers, was to receive a grant called Vandalia extending far beyond what was supposed to be the westernmost frontier. If Virginians followed regulations, they would be left behind.

Dunmore consequently stretched his instructions to the limit and beyond. He allowed land grants to be issued *in case* it was ever legal to settle the West; he accepted George Washington's argument that an exception in the regulations allowing British veterans to obtain land included provincial troops, which it was not at all clear London had meant; he evaded the prohibition against creating new counties in the West by labeling them "districts" instead; he fostered the Illinois-Wabash Company as a rival to the Walpole syndicate; and he withheld for years publication of new regulations radically revising the method of selling and the cost of land. Inevitably reprimands began to come from Great Britain until finally he was told of "his Majesty's just Displeasure" and advised that he was on dangerous ground. If other events had not intervened, he might well have been recalled for being too partial to Virginians.

It was the conflict with Pennsylvania over the region around Fort Pitt that brought out Dunmore's aggressive proclivities. On his journey to the area in the summer of 1773 he encouraged Virginia settlers not to recognize Pennsylvania's authority and bestowed his favor upon one of their most forceful leaders, Dr. John Connolly. Later even he had to warn Connolly that he was too ready to use violence. The following winter the two colonies established rival governments in the area: Pennsylvania the county of Westmoreland and Virginia the district of West Augusta. In January Pennsylvanians arrested Connolly, but on his release he raised a force and captured Fort Pitt, renaming it Fort Dunmore. For the moment there was a standoff. A complication was the rising hostility of Shawnee Indians in the area who refused to abide by treaties confining them to lands farther west. Brutal retaliation by both Virginians and Pennsylvanians upon innocent parties of Indians aggravated the situation. It became difficult to tell against whom war preparations were being made, each side fearing that the other was provoking the Indians to create a pretext for aggression.

In April 1774 Gov. John Penn offered to negotiate, but he proposed no significant concession and only recently had decreed death for any of Connolly's men caught resisting Pennsylvania authority. The Virginia Council rejected the offer as "a high Insult." With their concurrence, Dunmore requested troops from the legislature to fight the Indians, at the same time issuing a proclamation calling out the western militia "to repel any insult whatever." The government of Pennsylvania, he declared, was obstructing "his Majesty's Government . . . under my administration," and—almost as an afterthought—there was "danger of annoyance from the Indians also." Months later Lord Dartmouth, secretary of state for the colonies, wrote in astonishment, "I must observe to your Lordship that your Proclamation . . . implies too strongly the Necessity of exerting a Military Force, & breathes too much a Spirit of Hostility, that ought not to be encouraged in Matters of Civil Dispute between the Subjects of the same State."

Fortunately the burgesses, too, concluded that Dunmore was hankering to go to war with Gov. Penn and, to the distress of Washington and others sincerely concerned about the Indian situation, refused to supply the troops that Dunmore wanted. There were also some who felt that Virginia ought to husband its resources in view of the increasing tension with Great Britain.

Dunmore thereupon mounted an Indian campaign based entirely upon western militia. He left Williamsburg in July 1774 to assume personal command because, he said, the divisiveness on the frontier rendered it unwise to trust another leader. Yet his departure was only shortly after the imperial crisis had peaked in Virginia, when he dissolved the General Assembly because of its defiance of parliamentary authority. The cause of the crisis went back a year and a half when Parliament had attempted to rescue the financially distressed British East India Company by rebating all taxes on tea shipped to the colonies to reduce prices and encourage sales there. The only exception was the levy known as the Townshend duty, which Parliament had imposed in 1767 to help pay for colonial defense and administration. Americans who had consistently opposed this tax as unconstitutional now felt that they were being bribed to abandon their stand with the promise of cheaper tea.

The response of some in December 1773 was the Boston Tea Party, during which the offending chests of tea were thrown into Boston harbor. In retaliation, the British ministry ordered the port closed to trade until Bostonians reimbursed the company for its loss and altered the Massachusetts government to give royal authorities greater control. When the Virginia House of Burgesses indicated its sympathies by appointing the day on which Boston was to be shut, June 1, 1774, as a day of fast and prayer, Dunmore dissolved them. Most burgesses simply walked down the street in Williamsburg to the Raleigh Tavern, where, in extralegal sessions on May 26 and 27, they urged Virginians not to import or buy British goods and called for annual meetings of all the colonies in a continental congress to deliberate "the united interests of America." A few days later, when a proposal arrived from Boston to include in the boycott exports to Britain as well as imports, those burgesses still in town summoned a provincial convention to meet in August to consider expanding the prohibition.

For the moment, emotions remained under control. Having taken their stand, the burgesses played watch and wait. On the night of the Raleigh Tavern resolution, May 27, they went ahead with a ball at the Capitol that they had long been planning in honor of Lady Dunmore. The previous February the governor had finally brought her over with all their children, except their youngest son who was judged too little to travel. Captivated by Lady Dunmore's beauty and charm, already renowned in Europe, the burgesses did not forget their social obligations merely because her husband had dissolved them the day before.

Three weeks later, however, tension had mounted sufficiently for the Council to reverse its advice to dissolve the assembly. The Council now recommended that the governor hold elections for a new legislature. The members were especially concerned because the early dissolution had prevented extending the schedules of fees for public officials, without which the courts could not function. Dunmore, chiding them for their inconsistency and opining that another legislature would probably be as obstreperous as its predecessor, nonetheless set the next meeting of the assembly on August 11. But for whatever reason, by early July he had changed his mind and, postponing the session, headed west, leaving imperial affairs behind.

Dunmore's first war was a great success. The governor led a column of 1,300 men via Winchester and Wheeling to the confluence of the Hocking and Ohio rivers, which he reached about the first of October 1775. Another column of equal size under Col. Andrew Lewis of Augusta County marched from the Greenbrier River to Point Pleasant, at the mouth of the Great Kanawha River in modern West Virginia. There the main body of Shawnee under Chief Cornstalk attacked in force on October 10. Lewis's men took heavy casualties but eventually drove off the Indians. With Lewis following a few days behind, Dunmore led the way across the Ohio River toward the main Indian villages at Chillicothe, near which he established Camp Charlotte, named for both his wife and his queen. Faced with an overwhelming invasion, Cornstalk agreed to peace in the treaty of Camp Charlotte on October 19. On December 4 Dunmore returned to Williamsburg in triumph.

To crown his laurels, the day before he reached the capital, Lady

The Governor's Palace at Williamsburg. *Courtesy of the Colonial Williamsburg Foundation.*

Dunmore gave birth to a daughter, whom the parents christened Virginia. The only caveat against the governor's acclaim was from some of Lewis's men who felt that the terms of his treaty were too lenient in not excluding the Indians from lands north of the Ohio River as well as south of it. But it is not likely that this was the result of imperial strategy on Dunmore's part, since only the lands to the south had been in dispute at the beginning of the war.

Although Dunmore had occasionally expressed the fear gaining currency in Great Britain that settlement of the West would undermine British rule, his concern seemed to waver, depending on how feasible expansion—and profits—appeared to be. While in New York, where speculation in land was for the moment not in the West, he had warned the ministry that the Ohio Valley was too far from the sea for the British navy to control or British commerce to penetrate, thus encouraging local American manufactures, native competition, and economic independence. Later in Virginia, where there was readier access to the Ohio, he used the same argument to excuse moderate expansion. Virginians were so restless and mobile, he told London, that it was impossible to prevent migration beyond the mountains. Either Britain cooperated in hope of maintaining control or the inhabitants would fall into savagery or establish "a set of Democratic Governments of their own." Perhaps subconsciously he was revealing his own analysis of the troubles within the empire.

But for the moment in Williamsburg, at a ball he gave at the Palace on January 19, 1775, the day of his daughter's christening and the queen's birthday, Dunmore stood at the pinnacle of his fame in Virginia. "He is as popular as a Scotsman can be amongst weak prejudiced people" was the wry comment of a fellow Scot, merchant James Parker of Norfolk.

III

ONCE back in Williamsburg, Dunmore plunged into work to catch up with his duties and the imperial situation. He must have had the record of the August Convention in Williamsburg rushed to him in the West, for he dispatched from Frederick County a brief one-page notification of the meeting to Lord Dartmouth just seven days after the Convention had adjourned. Otherwise he sent to London only routine communications that gave insufficient account of the increasing restlessness in the colony. At meetings called during the summer of 1774 to elect assembly and convention delegates, many counties had expressed sympathy for the Bostonians; some sent off contributions to the captive city. When it met, the Virginia Convention expanded the boycott on British trade to include exports, and in October the first Continental Congress extended Virginia's example to all colonies, proscribing imports after November 1774 and exports after September 1775. During the fall county committees in Virginia formed to enforce these prohibitions, in some instances recruiting volunteer military companies and stockpiling arms.

All of this activity Dunmore summarized for Dartmouth in a fifty-page report dated Christmas Eve 1774. Yet, significantly, he devoted four-fifths of the letter to defending his land grants in the West and his machinations against Gov. Penn. His advice to Dartmouth with regard to the growing resistence was simply to take the Virginians at their word. They had already closed the courts—in his view, to escape payment of debts to Great Britain—so suspend the entire government, set up a blockade to enforce their own ban on British trade, and see who weakened first. The opposition's apparent strength, he said, was only because the county committees and volunteer companies were overawing the loyal majority. The lower classes would soon see that the rich had the means to avoid the boycott, and the oppressiveness of the enforcement committees would sow dissension.

Dartmouth thus knew little of developments in Virginia for six crucial months during which the ministry pushed steadfastly ahead with its plans to bring Boston to heel. Nothing challenged their vital assumption that colonies to the south would not rally to Massachusetts's side, allowing them to confront that colony alone. Dartmouth learned in July 1774 of Dunmore's dissolution of the Virginia legislature for proclaiming a day of fast. His immediate reaction was alarm that Virginia might set the pace for other colonies as it had in the past. But after that, there was little news other than the cryptic outline of the Convention's meeting, which he received in October.

Not until February 10 did Dunmore's voluminous report arrive. The secretary was shaken. "The steps which have been pursued in the different Counties of Virginia to carry into execution the Resolutions of the General Congress," he wrote to Dunmore a month later, "are of so extraordinary a nature that I am at a loss for words to express the criminality of them, and my surprise that the People should be so infatuated as tamely to submit to acts of such tyranny and oppression." He would read the letter to Parliament, he said, and expected that Virginia's trade would be interdicted as was Boston's, just as Dunmore recommended.

Dunmore himself, however, was unable to follow his own advice to leave punitive action to the navy. For one reason, it was not his nature to be so patient. For another, by mid-March he had received two instructions sent by Dartmouth to all governors, one ordering them to "take the most effectual measures for arresting, detaining, and securing any Gunpowder, or any sort of Arms or Ammunition which may be attempted to be imported into the Province under your Government" and the other to prevent the election of delegates to the second Continental Congress. These directives were circulars dispatched to all governors and were in no sense intended to bear specifically on Virginia. Gen. Thomas Gage in Boston, on the other hand, received direct marching orders that led to the battles of Lexington and Concord.

But a strict reading of the circulars could construe them as clear orders to act. Indeed, when news of their contents leaked out, the colonists saw in them positive evidence of an extensive conspiracy to arrest their leaders and send them to Great Britain for trial. Yet apart from these instructions and one other communication in May, authorizing the reconvening of the assembly, Dunmore received no directions at all until December 1775, as he quite justly and bitterly complained. What he did, despite his opponents' belief that he was acting in conformity to some great plan, he did entirely on his own.

Suspicion and tension mounted through the early months of 1775. Fearful that Dunmore might try to arrest them, the second Virginia Convention in March met in St. John's Church in Richmond, out of his reach. The climax of the session was the adoption of Patrick Henry's resolution to place the colony "in a posture of Defense," in support of which he delivered his inspired "Give me liberty or give me death" oration. Recruitment of volunteer companies accelerated, and arms were gathered.

It was this development that determined Dunmore to remove the small amount of gunpowder stored in the public magazine in Williamsburg before agitators seized it, as indeed some were planning to do. A body of marines from H.M.S. *Magdalen*, moored a few miles away at Burwell's Ferry on the James River, took the powder under cover of darkness early on April 21. They were seen, and by morning an angry crowd collected at the market green ready to storm the Governor's Palace. Luckily for Dunmore, Speaker Peyton Randolph of the House of Burgesses and cooler heads among the city fathers persuaded the mob to let them remonstrate vigorously with the governor. Tempers remained fiery, and the next day Dunmore showed how far he would go when in a fit of rage he threatened to turn the slaves against their masters.

The danger to Dunmore grew as news of what he had done spread through the colony. At Fredericksburg, volunteer companies numbering some 600 men who had gathered for training debated a whole day whether to march on Williamsburg. Magnifying the situation was news of the British attempt to seize New England leaders and gunpowder stored outside Boston, resulting in the defeat of royal troops at the battles of Lexington and Concord on April 19. None doubted that the similarity was more than coincidental. About this time Dunmore sent his wife and children to H.M.S. *Fowey* at Yorktown and prepared to defend the Palace. But again Peyton Randolph, George Washington, Richard Henry Lee, and Edmund Pendleton—all members of the Virginia congressional delegation—persuaded the Fredericksburg army to disband and for the moment to leave the struggle with Great Britain to Congress.

One congressional delegate, however, was not so easily mollified. Patrick Henry was with about 150 volunteers at Hanover County Courthouse, where he persuaded the county committee to let him lead a raid to force Dunmore to pay for the powder even by capturing royal officials if need be. He came within ten miles of the capital city before Carter Braxton, Robert Carter Nicholas, and others persuaded him to accept a bill of exchange for the value of the powder in the name of the Virginia Convention. Because Dunmore then declared Henry an outlaw, volunteer companies escorted him to the Maryland border, where that colony's companies took over to lead him along a hero's path all the way to the next session of Congress in Philadelphia. Only then did Dunmore dare let his family come home from Yorktown.

The governor was surprised by the uproar he had caused. Removal of the powder "was intended to have been done privately," he wrote Dartmouth. He had told the secretary in his December report that the apparent extent of unrest in the colony was because loyal subjects were intimidated by the county committees; now he was even more convinced that the trouble stemmed from a few firebrands like Henry. He would not admit to himself that bungling the raid on the public magazine had tumbled him so easily from his recent height of popularity, particularly in the West. There he continued to keep in close touch with William Preston of Botetourt and later Montgomery County and others over the attempt of North Carolina speculators under Richard Henderson to advance rival claims in the Kentucky area, and, while the March Convention was in session, had issued a proclamation designed to thwart Henderson. Despite the disturbances, Dunmore also continued to issue land grants to those with whom he was associated in the West, including one to George Washington even after the latter had been appointed commander-in-chief of the Continental Army.

But Dunmore's name was ruined in Virginia. On April 29 the *Virginia Gazette* published excerpts from his report of the previous December which Lord Dartmouth had read to Parliament. Fortunately for Dunmore, Dartmouth had not revealed the portions recommending a blockading fleet, which remained unknown to Virginians for a while longer. But what was made available sufficed to paint him an unbelievable villain who was trying to undermine Congress's efforts to negotiate the imperial crisis. Since Congress had not heard from its petitions to the king and Parliament the October before, moderates were still urging calm so as not to jeopardize success. Now, despite their pacifying efforts, Dunmore was discovered describing colonial resistance as completely illegal and implying that the opposition in no way represented Virginia opinion and would quickly collapse. Just when he was expected to be impressing upon the ministry the unity and determination of the colonists in the hope of persuading the government to compromise, he was found giving the British reason not to heed American petitions and to risk a stiff-necked policy.

For most of May an uneasy calm settled over Virginia. Dunmore received orders from Dartmouth to reconvene the assembly to consider the offer of the prime minister, Lord North, to let the colonies collect their own taxes if they would guarantee amounts specified by Parliament. Dunmore set June 1 as the day for the assembly to meet. Peyton Randolph, who had been elected president of the Continental Congress, resigned to return to his post as speaker of the House of Burgesses. Distrustful of the governor, volunteer companies met Randolph outside of town to escort him into the Virginia capital, and the Williamsburg company posted guards about his house. Nonetheless, both Randolph and Thomas Jefferson were concerned that Lord North's conciliatory offer would win enough support to be accepted, even though it made no real concession to the principle of "no taxation without representation."

The surface calm lasted only a few days into June. The weekend after the assembly met, several young men trying to break into the Williamsburg magazine in order to arm themselves were greeted by the blast of a shotgun rigged to go off at the tripping of a spring. Although the only two casualties were slight, everywhere Dunmore was denounced as a would-be murderer. In Philadelphia even Edmund Pendleton, a lawyer not given to violent words, brought up the possibility of assassination. Over the next two or three days the assembly and the governor exchanged recriminations. A mob rioted at the powder magazine; and at the rumor that royal marines were coming from Yorktown the city's volunteer company mobilized. Dunmore may also have learned that John Pinckney's *Virginia Gazette* was about to publish the missing sections of his Christmas letter to Dartmouth, in which he called for a punitive expedition against Virginia. Deciding that in this atmosphere the wisest course was to leave, he led his little band in the morning darkness of June 8 through the Palace park toward Yorktown.

IV

RETREAT proved worse for Dunmore than attack. His flight polarized political opinion in Virginia even more than had his raid on the public magazine. Not only might the simultaneous appearance of the *Otter* in York River be a harbinger of the fleet they now knew he had summoned. But by saying that he was fleeing for his life, he lumped moderates like the treasurer, Robert Carter Nicholas, who had been counseling patience, with the Patrick Henrys, forcing them to face the possibility that Henry was right after all, petitions and soft words had no effect. Nicholas chaired a committee of the burgesses to answer the implication of Dunmore's charges that everyone in the opposition had been planning to rebel all along. The resulting resolution gave a highly partisan version of events over the past year, emphasizing the calm reasonableness of Virginians. It was as if all had actually followed Nicholas's advice.

Ignoring the hot words being spoken about Dunmore even by members of the assembly, the committee elicited testimony from whatever witnesses they could find that Dunmore and Capt. Foy had walked about Williamsburg without fear until the eve of their flight. The committee denied Dunmore's allegation that Virginians had closed the courts to avoid paying their legitimate debts to Great Britain. The sole reason, the burgesses reiterated, was that Dunmore had dissolved the previous assembly before it could enact a fee schedule. The committee also rejected the assertion that the raising of volunteer companies was intended to intimidate friends of the crown. The companies, they declared, were formed by gentlemen "desirous of perfecting themselves in military exercise" when they realized how poorly the governor had been enforcing the militia laws, even though "a person of great influence" was advising the arming of slaves. As for trade restrictions and county committees to enforce them, these were entirely the fault of the British, for they would not have been necessary except for British attacks on colonial liberty.

Fundamentally Nicholas completely agreed with the Henrys of the colony that Virginia's liberties were in need of defense; their disagreement was solely over means. The note of wounded innocence permeating the long resolution attested to the rising despair of Nicholas and his kind and their determination that no one would ever be able to say that they had not tried their best for peace or had been the first to resort to violence. They returned to this theme again and again; even their final Resolution for Independence would reaffirm it.

The assembly spent the remaining three weeks of its life trying to persuade Dunmore that it was safe to return to Williamsburg and resume normal government, or, if royal authority was to fail, to be certain that the members would not be blamed. The burgesses carried on the usual routine of legislation, sending papers and messages to Yorktown as if the governor just happened to be temporarily out of town, but declined to meet him as a body on board ship. At one point they even submitted a standard supply request for 2,000 stand of arms, 5 tons of powder, and 20 of lead to restock the powder magazine, and another time asked if it would be all right to take his collection of arms in the hallway of the Palace! At length Dunmore made them face reality by refusing to sign a bill that was crucial to the final settlement of the Indian war. Either the assembly ignored his veto—and, by appointing commissioners to conclude the treaty without his consent, usurped executive authority for the first time—or fighting would break out again on the frontier.

Eventually, too, people outside the assembly were becoming impatient with the sparring with the governor. The news of his flight brought volunteers to protect Williamsburg from the expected invasion. Soon there were about 200 armed men in town, mostly young, who acted as if they were on a lark; "We appear rather invited to feast than fight," one observed. Their officers, who were elected, were unable to control them, and the number of incidents began to increase. Three times they raided the Governor's Palace and once shot up Dunmore and a small party at his York County plantation, Porto Bello. They set up quarters in the Palace and, after the General Assembly adjourned on June 24, in the Capitol as well. Later, to create a little excitement, they rounded up any royal official they thought might have some of the crown's money on hand until finally the next Convention made them stop.

26

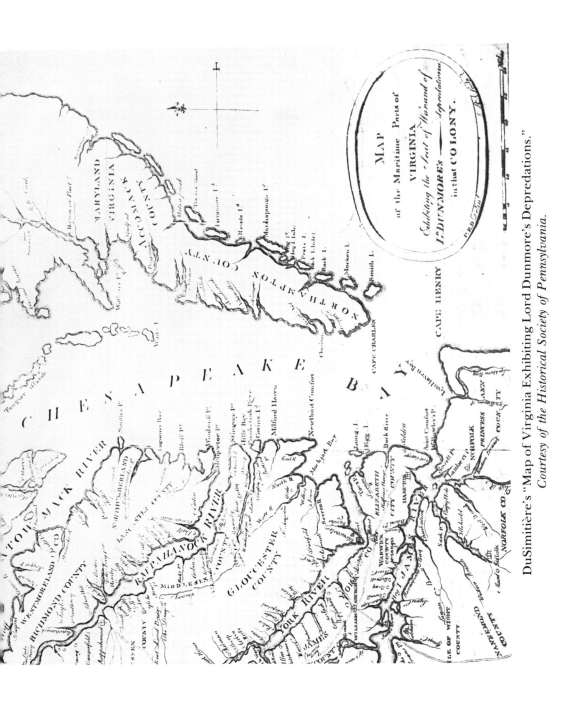

DuSimitière's "Map of Virginia Exhibiting Lord Dunmore's Depredations."
Courtesy of the Historical Society of Pennsylvania.

27

Toward the end of the month Dunmore sent his wife and family home to Great Britain on board the schooner *Magdalen*, which he obtained for the trip by countermanding the orders of the British naval commander, Adm. Samuel Graves, in Boston, who had assigned the vessel to Delaware Bay. With them went the Rev. Thomas Gwatkin, a member of the faculty of the College of William and Mary and tutor of the governor's eldest son, Lord Fincastle. Earlier in his career at William and Mary, Gwatkin had once earned the official approbation of the House of Burgesses for his determined opposition to the appointment of an Anglican bishop in the colonies, whom many feared would be a tool of the British. But he had fallen into popular disfavor in 1774 by refusing to preach on the fast day in support of Boston, although he wrote the sermon for the occasion. Thereafter, he declined to participate in the resistance movement. The alleged visit of a group of armed men to his rooms at the college in May 1775 hastened a decision to return to England, where out of gratitude for his services Dunmore did all he could to help him reestablish himself.

Two weeks later, on July 14, Capt. Foy and his wife took advantage of the *Fowey's* sailing to return to New York and from there to England. The parting of the governor and his subordinate was not happy. Had Virginians known, they would have enjoyed the irony. To them Foy was cut from the same cloth as his master; if anything, he was more arrogant and condescending. A member of a prominent mercantile family of Bristol, England, he had caned a shopkeeper on the streets of Williamsburg and left few unaware that he was one of those who had received commendations at the battle of Minden in 1759, which for the most part had been a total disgrace for the British. He was even mentioned by name for his heroism in Tobias Smollett's account of the battle in his popular history of England. Earlier Dunmore had directed considerable patronage to him, irritating native aspirants in the process; and after Foy's marriage in 1773 to Hannah Van Horne of New York, the governor and Lady Dunmore had both tried in vain to find him a post in that city.

As Dunmore's troubles multiplied, however, he apparently attempted to block any transfer in order to keep his assistant by his side. Seeing no future in that and resenting the lack of advancement after five years of faithful service, Foy departed with the bitter remark, "I am no longer interested in the fate of Lord Dunmore." The governor apparently did not reciprocate, for when they met again in England,

Dunmore introduced him to the king. Foy returned to America on the staff of Baron Riedesel, a commander of German mercenaries in British employ, whom Americans knew as the "Hessians" even though many came from provinces other than Hesse. Riedesel, for example, was a Brunswickian. Later, Foy became secretary to Gen. Sir Guy Carleton, governor of Canada.

Within several weeks of Foy's departure, Dunmore lost another supporter, the attorney general, John Randolph. Educated in England and renowned for his brilliance in law, Randolph was a pillar of the Virginia intelligentsia. As fellow violinists and bibliophiles, he and Jefferson were particularly close. In their final correspondence, in which they agreed to disagree, the respect of each for the other intellectually is manifest. A year before, with Dunmore absent in the West, Randolph had stood up for the empire and criticized, in an exchange of pamphlets with Robert Carter Nicholas, the Virginia assembly's resolutions in support of Boston. Later, Dunmore used his membership on the Board of Visitors of William and Mary to have Randolph returned as the college's delegate to the House of Burgesses to insure that there was at least one imperial spokesman in that body.

The close collaboration brought retribution from the populace. There were slanderous rumors, for example, that behind the alliance was the fact that Randolph's daughter, Susanna, was Dunmore's mistress, and the night after the Randolphs left, a mob ransacked their home in Williamsburg. A final letter from the attorney general to his son, Edmund, who was an aide to Gen. Washington, begging him to return to Williamsburg to care for the family's interests, reveals the anguish felt by families like the Randolphs, Byrds, and Blands, who had members on both sides of the war. In England, the Randolphs stayed first at Dunmore's home in Scotland and then joined the colony of eminent American loyalists on Brompton Row, London, where John Randolph became one of the principal lobbyists for the loyalist cause in England.

Meanwhile, Dunmore was preparing to meet force with force. During July and August he collected a small fleet at Portsmouth. He commandeered two merchantmen, the *Eilbeck*, which he rigged for twenty-two guns but on which he was never able to emplace more than seven, and the fourteen-gun *William*, on which he first set up his headquarters. Later he moved to the *Eilbeck*, renaming it after himself.

In addition, he could usually count on the help of two royal naval ships plus their several tenders. The latter, armed with swivel guns and a couple of three- or four-pound cannon, were particularly effective harassing fishing and coastwise vessels plying their trade in Hampton Roads. At first the naval ships were the fourteen-gun sloop *Otter* and the twenty-gun *Mercury*, which had come in regular rotation for the *Fowey*. But Capt. John MacCartney of the *Mercury* fell out with the governor because MacCartney accepted a dinner invitation from the president of the Council, Thomas Nelson of Yorktown, who had succeeded his late brother, William, in that post. In addition, MacCartney refused to harbor escaped slaves as a general policy but insisted on first satisfying himself that their masters were criminals whose property was subject to confiscation. Furious at such independence, Dunmore complained to Adm. Graves in Boston, who ordered MacCartney put under arrest. Subsequently the charges were dropped. The governor was beginning to acquire with the military the reputation of being headlong and a bit of a nuisance. Eventually, too, Dunmore came to regret his impulsiveness with regard to MacCartney when the smaller eighteen-gun sloop *King's Fisher* arrived to replace the heavier *Mercury*.

During the summer, the British commander in America, Lt. Gen. Thomas Gage, responded to Dunmore's pleas for an army by ordering the transfer of units of the 14th Regiment from St. Augustine, Florida, and Providence Island in the Caribbean. Sixty men arrived on July 31, but, when Dunmore sent the *Otter* for more, Gov. Patrick Tonyn of Florida refused to release them until he obtained replacements for fear of an uprising there.

About this time, too, Dunmore began to lay plans to capitalize on the friendships that he had built in the West. His agent, Dr. John Connolly had been negotiating from mid-June to early July with Indian chieftains at Fort Pitt to conclude the peace treaty resulting from the governor's previous campaign. Some westerners were already suspicious of Connolly and petitioned Congress to have commissioners from Virginia and Pennsylvania intervene. But when James Wood, the investigator appointed by the Virginia Convention, reported that there was no evidence Connolly had used the conference for Dunmore's purposes, the Convention voted Connolly their thanks instead. Connolly nevertheless felt that he had subtly swayed the Indians. He also apparently misinterpreted an incident in the continuing Virginia-Pennsylvania border feud. Kidnapped by

Pennsylvanians in the middle of the conference, he was forcibly rescued by Virginia frontiersmen, whom he concluded he could rely upon in other enterprises as well.

After the conference Connolly set out for Norfolk, which he reached late in August 1775, to unfold a daring strategy to Dunmore. Later when he put his adventures on paper, he related how on this trip he had used the Convention's commendation to escape arrest at Warm Springs and had slipped past sentinels at Williamsburg in a blinding rainstorm. The plan was that he would go to Boston to obtain Gen. Gage's permission to lead an expedition from Detroit into the Ohio country where he would raise reinforcements among the loyalists and rendezvous with Dunmore along the Potomac River the next spring. The juncture of their two forces would isolate Virginia from the northern colonies and force its rapid surrender.

Connolly was able to reach Boston and gain Gage's consent but no troops. The best that Gage, who was himself besieged by Washington's army, could do was to give Connolly letters to officers at Detroit and to the deputy superintendent of Indian affairs at Fort Pitt, Alexander McKee, to aid him in every way possible. To make matters worse, Connolly had to return to Virginia by sea because Continental troops invading Canada that winter blocked the overland route to Detroit. On the way he stopped at Newport, Rhode Island, where a servant deserted and informed Washington's secret agents of the plan.

Meanwhile, a letter written to a supposedly loyal supporter at Fort Pitt, John Gibson, alerted rebel authorities in the South. Delayed again by illness in Virginia, it was November before Connolly set off through Maryland for Fort Pitt in the company of two other loyalists, Dr. J. F. D. Smyth and Alexander Cameron. By then the countryside had been warned, and he was taken prisoner with his companions at Hagerstown, Maryland, on November 19. Incriminating documents found in a secret compartment of his luggage consigned him to prison for the rest of the war. Unfortunately for Dunmore, Connolly's plan came to light just as letters to Gen. Gage from John Stuart, the superintendent for Indian affairs in the southern department, advocating limited use of Indians in the war were captured. Dunmore stood convicted of raising western "savages" as well as slaves against Virginia.

By September there was open warfare in the Hampton Roads area. After a hurricane howled through the Tidewater early in the month,

Pinckney's *Virginia Gazette* regaled its readers with a story of Dunmore tumbling into the water but assured them that "those who are born to be h____d will never be DROWNED." High winds drove the *Mercury* aground off Norfolk and one of the *Otter's* tenders, the *Liberty*, off Hampton. The British struggled for ten days before they freed the larger ship; the other was lost to the rebels. Capt. Matthew Squire of the *Otter*, who was aboard his tender until the last moment, escaped only by jumping into the water and hiding in the woods overnight. Mortified, he returned with the *Otter* a week later, threatening to bombard Hampton unless reparations were made. One hundred Virginia volunteers under Maj. James Innes hastened down from Williamsburg. The Virginians released all of the tender's crew that had been captured except two runaway slaves but refused to return any of its equipment unless Squire gave up Joseph Harris, a Hampton slave who was the pilot of the *Otter*. The British reply was to clamp a tight blockade on Hampton Roads.

All this while John Hunter Holt, editor of the *Virginia Gazette* of Norfolk and nephew of another John Holt, a whig printer in New York, kept up a rapid fire of epithets and insults at Dunmore and his allies. The treasonable activities of the governor's noble ancestors were duly noted, and Capt. Squire was ridiculed as a result of his recent escapade. Finding his orders to halt laughed at, Squire finally landed a detachment on the afternoon of September 30 to seize the offender. Although Holt was able to hide and escape, the troops carried the press and two assistants aboard the *Eilbeck*. In November, Dunmore and his editor, Hector MacAlester, brought out the first issue of their own *Gazette,* which they published sporadically at least until March. Later the assistants were sent with their equipment to help the British army publish newspapers in New York and Philadelphia.

The episode badly injured Norfolk in the opinion of the rest of the colony, for a hundred or more spectators lined up to watch with no attempt to stop the soldiers. When the local militia colonel, Matthew Phripp, sounded the alarm, none of the men who responded would go near the British. Phripp resigned in anger. Nor did anyone interfere when the soldiers returned a couple of weeks later for more ink and paper. Other Virginians began to mutter that something had to be done about Norfolk.

Little more than a generation old, Norfolk reflected changing times in Virginia. A constantly increasing grain trade bound for

Philadelphia and the West Indies flowed through its harbor, and Scottish factors residing in its environs directed tobacco operations for large firms in Glasgow, such as those of William Cunninghame, Alexander Speirs, and John Glassford. By 1770 Scots had captured about 50 percent of the tobacco trade. Inevitably there was friction, which was exacerbated by the dubious reputation of Scots among Englishmen everywhere. While to men like Dunmore the stigma of earlier treasons may well have been a special goad to prove their allegiance to the crown, to Virginians it seemed as if the Scots were up to their tory tricks again.

Not all inhabitants of Norfolk were tories, as John Holt proved. When John Schaw, one of Dunmore's commissaries, turned in a resident for wearing a hunting shirt, the uniform of the new Virginia army, he barely escaped being tarred and feathered. But once British guns came to bear on the town, men like Holt and Phripp lost out. In a protest to Dunmore about the seizure of Holt's press, the Norfolk Common Council emphasized that the populace had not resisted, to which the governor cynically replied that it was for "some other reason" than their loyalty.

Gradually the indictment against the city lengthened. To the horror of leaders in Williamsburg, Matthew Phripp went over to Dunmore, although eventually he returned and was able to acquit himself on the ground that the British had intimidated his family. Intercepted letters revealed that merchants anticipating an invasion fleet were ordering tens of thousands of pounds' worth of goods to supply it. Most damaging, some were contacting influential friends in Great Britain to obtain posts of condemned Virginia officials, while some firms were advancing the government funds for the campaign in expectation of compensation from confiscated estates in Virginia. "I intend with many others to . . . spend the Remainder of my life in a Retirement . . . near to you," wrote one Britisher to his brother in Norfolk. Jefferson expressed the feeling of many when he paraphrased the cry of ancient Romans, "Carthage must be destroyed," in a letter to his friend John Page, "delenda est Norfolk."

Throughout the fall the Committee of Safety, which the Virginia Convention had appointed under the chairmanship of Edmund Pendleton as an interim executive for the colony, gathered about 2,000 men around Williamsburg in preparation for the campaign against Dunmore. The Convention had replaced the obstreperous volunteers that had caused so much trouble during the summer with two regiments under regular military discipline. There also were minutemen who were obligated to train periodically to be ready for service on an instant's notice, as well as the traditional militia. After a bitter debate over his lack of military experience, Patrick Henry narrowly won election as colonel of the 1st Regiment and commander-in-chief of Virginia forces, to the disgruntlement of old soldiers like Hugh Mercer of Fredericksburg. Col. William Woodford was placed in command of the 2nd Regiment. To supply these units Virginia was fortunate in that it was a rich agricultural province and, for the first few months at least, found enough on merchants' shelves and in the soldiers' own homes to meet minimum needs. Gunpowder was the principal item that had to be brought in from abroad.

Suddenly on October 12 the governor launched a rapid series of raids to check the Virginians' war effort. At various landings and shipyards around Norfolk were cannon left over from the French and Indian War during which the city had outfitted and armed many privateers. Already the rebels had secluded many of these, but acting on excellent intelligence from loyalist supporters, Dunmore and his men uncovered the hiding places.

In the first sortie Dunmore and Capt. Samuel Leslie marched a few miles outside Norfolk with a small detachment of the British 14th Regiment and destroyed seventeen cannon and captured two more belonging to Joseph Hutchings. Learning a few days later that there was a large cache of arms including a shipment of powder recently brought in from the West Indies at Kemp's Landing, Dunmore launched another sudden attack. On October 17 he sailed quickly up the east branch of the Elizabeth River, landed, and moved swiftly inland. Nearby 200 militia commanded by Hutchings were drilling. They ran into the woods at Dunmore's approach. He captured several, including a convention delegate, William Robinson. The British pillaged part of the town, destroying a number of small arms, but discovered that the cannon and powder had been safely evacuated by the rebels a short time before.

Returning to Norfolk on October 18, Dunmore rested only a day before he sent off Lt. John Batut with a patrol to search out twenty more cannon in another hideaway a short distance from the city. Similar excursions on the succeeding two days brought the total number of cannon destroyed or taken to seventy-two in addition to many smaller arms and quantities of ball and shot, which "I believe," Dunmore reported to London, "is all the Military Stores in this neighbourhood that could be of any Service to the Rebels." Capt.

Leslie, however, took a more pessimistic view in his report. The quantity of arms destroyed, he wrote, "is a proof that it would require a very large force to subdue this Colony."

After these successes Dunmore turned his attention across the water to Hampton. During the night of October 25 Capt. Squire drew up a squadron of five ships before the town, but a barricade of sunken vessels in the channel prevented him from approaching close enough to burn the town as he announced that he intended to do. He landed a beach party under cover of darkness to raid some houses and take away a slave at Mills Creek and, the next day, after a heavy exchange of fire with two companies and some militia under Capt. George Nicholas and Capt. George Lyne, succeeded in burning the farmhouse at Cooper's plantation at the mouth of the Hampton River.

That night the British finally hacked their way through the barricade, but by then Col. Woodford had arrived with a company of riflemen from Williamsburg. From the cover of houses along the main street the riflemen poured such heavy fire on the British that they had to withdraw. In such close sea-to-shore engagements, the accuracy of Virginia riflemen repeatedly proved more than a match for the navy by preventing the sailors from remaining on deck long enough to fire their guns. In the retreat, another tender of the *Otter*, the *Hawk*, went aground. Ten of its crew were captured and its skipper killed. Dunmore suffered at least one other killed and several wounded. The Virginians had no casualties.

The Committee of Safety, under criticism from Congress for not doing something about Dunmore, had already laid its plans when the attack on Hampton intervened. All traffic to or from Norfolk and Portsmouth had been halted except by special pass, and the committee issued orders for the 2nd Regiment to move across the James River. Ordinarily Patrick Henry as colonel of the 1st Regiment would have been the commander in the field, but as the weeks in camp had not diminished concern about his military inexperience, Edmund Pendleton and a majority of the committee decided to bypass him for Woodford despite the political risks involved. By November 7 Woodford had moved a few of his men across the river at Jamestown when the *King's Fisher* and several tenders appeared on patrol. Virginia riflemen were able to keep the British from damaging the ferries, but Woodford was forced to move upstream to Sandy Point, where the main body was finally able to cross after beating off a British sloop. By then it was November 19.

The delay was unfortunate. On the night of November 14

Dunmore was reconnoitering in the vicinity of Great Bridge, where a large force of North Carolinians had been reported. Meanwhile, Joseph Hutchings and Arthur Lawson were assembling the Princess Anne militia at Kemp's Landing. Finding no one at Great Bridge the next day but hearing of Hutchings's force, Dunmore marched on. Although the Virginians had time to set up an ambush, the inexperienced militia gave themselves away by firing too soon and fled. Five Virginians were killed, two drowned trying to escape, and eighteen were taken, including Hutchings, who, deserted by his men, was captured by one of his own slaves who had joined Dunmore. Lawson and a few others fled toward the North Carolina border, near which they were taken in their sleep. The British suffered only one casualty, a grenadier nicked in the knee. Dunmore then moved into Kemp's Landing and continued pillaging where he had left off.

Flushed with victory, Dunmore seized the occasion to raise the king's standard—an action proclaiming a state of rebellion and requiring all loyal subjects to help suppress it. To his chagrin he could not find a royal ensign and had to substitute regimental colors. He had already prepared a proclamation for the occasion which he had signed on November 7 but had kept in his pocket for a propitious moment. Undoubtedly he knew, too, of the king's own declaration to the same effect which had appeared in the last issue of the *Virginia Gazette*. But Dunmore went beyond this. Commanding supporters of government to join his ranks under penalty of law, he continued, "and I do farther declare all indented Servants, Negroes, or others (appertaining to Rebels) free, that are able and willing to bear Arms, they joining his Majesty's forces."

At last he had done it! He had finally carried out his threat to free the slaves. As an act of war his move was an obvious tactic, for Virginians long recognized the large number of slaves in their midst as their greatest military weakness. It had earlier been a matter of concern to Dunmore himself in planning imperial defense of the colony, and in the current controversy several British commentators had remarked that it was one reason not to worry about Virginia breaking away from the mother country. Writing from London a while before, William Lee even urged freeing the slaves before the British did.

Actually the decree merely summed up Dunmore's policy of several months past, which had already enticed many Negroes to his lines. But it enunciated that policy in final, official form; and, although

36

By His Excellency the Right Honorable JOHN Earl of DUNMORE, His
Majesty's Lieutenant and Governor General of the Colony and Dominion of
Virginia, and Vice Admiral of the same.

A PROCLAMATION.

AS I have ever entertained Hopes that an Accommodation might have
taken Place between Great-Britain and this Colony, without being
compelled by my Duty to this most disagreeable but now absolutely necessary
Step, rendered so by a Body of armed Men unlawfully assembled, firing on His
Majesty's Tenders, and the formation of an Army, and that Army now on
their March to attack His Majesty's Troops and destroy the well disposed Subjects of this Colony. To defeat such treasonable Purposes, and that all such
Traitors, and their Abettors, may be brought to Justice, and that the Peace, and
good Order of this Colony may be again restored, which the ordinary Course
of the Civil Law is unable to effect; I have thought fit to issue this my Proclamation, hereby declaring, that until the aforesaid good Purposes can be obtained, I do in Virtue of the Power and Authority to ME given, by His Majesty, determine to execute Martial Law, and cause the same to be executed
throughout this Colony: and to the end that Peace and good Order may the
sooner be restored, I do require every Person capable of bearing Arms, to resort
to His Majesty's STANDARD, or be looked upon as Traitors to His
Majesty's Crown and Government, and thereby become liable to the Penalty
the Law inflicts upon such Offences; such as forfeiture of Life, confiscation of
Lands, &c. &c. And I do hereby further declare all indented Servants, Negroes,
or others, (appertaining to Rebels,) free that are able and willing to bear Arms,
they joining His Majesty's Troops as soon as may be, for the more speedily
reducing this Colony to a proper Sense of their Duty, to His Majesty's
Crown and Dignity. I do further order, and require, all His Majesty's Leige
Subjects, to retain their Quitrents, or any other Taxes due or that may become
due, in their own Custody, till such Time as Peace may be again restored to this
at present most unhappy Country, or demanded of them for their former salu-
tary Purposes, by Officers properly authorised to receive the same.

GIVEN under my Hand on board the Ship WILLIAM, off Norfolk,
the 7th Day of November, in the sixteenth Year of His Majesty's Reign.

DUNMORE.

(GOD save the KING.)

Dunmore's Emancipation Proclamation. *Courtesy of the Virginia State Library,
Richmond.*

37

the records are not completely clear, it apparently drove William Byrd III, for one, who otherwise was quite sympathetic to the governor, to tender his services to the Convention—a not inconsiderable offer since he had commanded the 2nd Virginia Regiment in the French and Indian War. Virginia leaders turned him down only after careful consideration.

Humanitarian concern was not Dunmore's primary motive. He was a large slaveholder himself and carefully limited his proclamation to slaves of his opponents and then only to able-bodied males. In some cases, slaves of tories were turned back to their masters when they tried to enlist; others, however, were drafted. Dunmore was also indifferent to arranging exchanges for black soldiers who were captured. There is no evidence, on the other hand, to support the rumor the Virginians spread to discourage runaways that Dunmore sold Negro troops in the West Indies to raise money. Those who were still with him in the end went to New York. Several hundred blacks eventually joined his Ethiopian Regiment, under the command of William Byrd III's son, Thomas, a British army officer, including some free blacks, who later claimed compensation for land confiscated under antiloyalist laws. Many others tried to reach Dunmore's lines but failed. Those whom the Virginians took alive under arms were either sold in the West Indies and their masters compensated or sent to work in the lead mines or other public works. Despite many threats, few were executed.

Dunmore set up the king's standard on November 15. On the next morning about 100 of the militia who had fought against him took his oath of allegiance:

> Whereas a set of factious men under the names of Committees Conventions and Congresses have violently and under various pretenses usurped the legislative and executive powers of Government and are thereby endeavouring to overturn our Constitution and have incured [sic] the Guilt of actual Rebellion against our most gracious Sovereign, I, A.B., do therefore abjure all their Authority and solemnly promise in the presence of Almighty God to bear faith and true Allegiance to his sacred Majesty George 3d and will to the utmost of my power and ability support maintain and defend his Crown and dignity against all traiterous [sic] attempts and conspiracies whatsoever. So Help me God.

The same afternoon Dunmore marched back to Norfolk, where he erected the standard again, and received some 200 pledges of loyalty, including those of the mayor and aldermen. Norfolk welcomed him and his men enthusiastically. The price of red cloth from which to make badges for loyalists to distinguish themselves was said to have risen precipitously. It seemed as if he was correct, that if only a stand was taken, a small victory won, the people would regain confidence in the government and come to its support. Within a short time, more than 3,000 whites from the Norfolk-Portsmouth area were reported to have taken the oath.

The outpouring provided Dunmore with a promising little army. The recent arrival of additional men from the British 14th Regiment had brought his force of regulars to 175. Lt. Col. Jacob Ellegood of the county militia led about 600 men to his side and was immediately commissioned colonel of the new Queen's Own Loyal Regiment. James Parker, a well established Scottish merchant, became Dunmore's chief engineer, and his partner, Thomas MacKnight, was put in charge of fortifying the city. Neil Jamieson, the chief factor of Glassford & Co., was supply agent, and Hector McAlestor paymaster, while James Ingram became chief justice and John Brown vendue master of Dunmore's admiralty court for the condemnation of prizes taken at sea. The elderly Andrew Sprowle, unofficial leader of the Virginia merchant community for a generation, provided buildings for barracks.

Perhaps the most effective converts Dunmore made were John Goodrich and his sons, John, Jr., William, and Bartlett. Goodrich owned a plantation in Isle of Wight County, but was known primarily as a smuggler and sea captain in the West Indian trade. In July, Robert Carter Nicholas had hired the father and William to buy £5,000 worth of powder in the Caribbean, some of which William actually purchased from a British ship. The powder successfully arrived in Williamsburg, but the Goodriches also landed English goods disguised as Dutch to evade Congress's prohibition of imports from the mother country. Meanwhile Dunmore learned of the powder and with threats of retaliation found it not too difficult to win the family to his side.

The Goodriches' expert knowledge of Tidewater streams made them extremely valuable for leading foraging expeditions and lightning raids against isolated plantations and ship landings. Obviously fast talkers, they played a double game with the Committee of

39

Safety and the Virginia Convention for most of the winter, but eventually all were captured by the rebels and imprisoned. Proving equally adept as jailbreakers they escaped one by one to lead a small fleet of loyalist privateers up and down the coast from New Jersey to the Carolinas for the rest of the war. The family retired to England and Bermuda after the war, Bartlett at least "with a Capitall fortune."

Dunmore formally occupied the city of Norfolk on November 23 and put his men to work constructing a ring of fortifications from "river to river" that one observer estimated would have taken 5,000 men and 20 cannon to defend. Obviously Dunmore expected support and soon. Two days earlier Col. Woodford had been at Cobham in Surry County, when he heard a false rumor that Dunmore was marching to take Suffolk, and sent Lt. Col. Charles Scott with 215 men racing 35 miles in a single day to garrison it. Woodford's main force reached the town on the twenty-fifth.

The confrontation with the British came at Great Bridge, which guarded the only route across the Elizabeth River to Norfolk. Since the entrenchments around the city required many more men than Dunmore had, it was imperative that he keep the rebels from crossing the Elizabeth River and cutting the city off from the food supplies of Princess Anne and Norfolk counties until reinforcements arrived. On his previous excursion to Great Bridge he had built a small wooden fort that the Virginians derisively referred to as the "hogpen" and had garrisoned it with about 100 men, half of them black. By November 28, the advanced Virginia detachment under Scott was in position across the way and the firing began. Woodford arrived four days later.

The terrain at Great Bridge was ideal for defense. At that point in the river the main channel on both sides was lined with wide marshes. From the town on the south bank a causeway across which an attacking force could only move five or six abreast ran to an island on which there were several houses. The bridge itself spanned the main stream from the island to another causeway opposite, where the British fort with two four-pound cannon commanded the approach. Most of the planking on the bridge had been torn up. The Virginians, after pitching camp on the far side of town, constructed a barricade at the end of the main street and dug entrenchments along the bank to the northeast from which riflemen could sweep the bridge. At night they posted pickets on the island but withdrew them at daylight to protect them from British fire.

The stalemate lasted for over a week. Woodford, who had the reputation of being overly cautious, was pushed by his younger officers to attack, but declined because he lacked the cannon to reduce the fort and was short of ammunition. His plight worsened when tories sabotaged Bachelor Mill Dam preventing his wagons from crossing Deep Creek, the quickest route to Suffolk. Repeatedly he wrote to Williamsburg for bullet molds, powder, cannon, and enough blankets to issue each man two as protection against the raw winter weather. Informed that a group of North Carolinians was marching north with cannon, he sent a message urging them to hurry and to block Dunmore's retreat to the south. One company of Carolinians did arrive on December 3 but without cannon.

For several days most of the action was at a ford five or six miles downstream from Great Bridge. Both British and Virginians collected boats on opposite sides of the river and posted detachments to guard them. The day after Scott arrived, a small party of British attacked but were driven off. On December 3 Lt. Col. Edward Stevens with 100 men stole across a mile or so below the boats to surprise the British but gave themselves away by firing too soon. After a hot skirmish in which they killed two black soldiers and captured two more, Stevens's men withdrew. Three days later Scott tried again with a larger party. Once more the surprise was lost when the Virginians were seen by a supply wagon coming from Norfolk. A white and two blacks among the British were killed and two more blacks captured, but again the black company frustrated the attack. The Virginians suffered one wounded. Back at Great Bridge the firing was constant every day; the only action was a successful sally by a squad of black British troops on December 4 to burn five or six houses on the island in the middle of the river from which Woodford's men had been sniping at the British fort.

Despite the advantage of his position, it was Dunmore who broke the deadlock by attacking. His reason is not clear. Woodford heard afterward that an escaped slave told the governor that there were only a couple of hundred Virginians opposing him and subsequently elaborated the story to suggest that he had sent the man for that purpose. Virginians savored the irony of Dunmore being duped by a runaway black. But since Woodford was camped within sight of the British, more likely it was as Dunmore reported to London: he had learned that a body of North Carolinians was one day's march away with cannon that he knew his fort could not withstand.

The tactic in retrospect was foolhardy, virtually suicidal. Officers of the 14th Regiment advised against it. They had been sent to act as bodyguards for Dunmore and felt that only because he let his judgment be swayed by the pleading of merchants who feared the loss of their property were they in the position of having to defend Norfolk. Yet when their commander, Capt. Samuel Leslie, found on his arrival at the fort about three o'clock in the morning of December 9 that the black troops who were to create a diversion were guarding the ford downstream, too far away to help, he still elected to carry on. Then, because he had to let his men rest after their twelve-mile march through the night, he did not attack until just as reveille was beaten at the Virginian camp, eliminating whatever surprise there was in his favor. Both he and Dunmore apparently were too confident that untried rebels, however well positioned, would not stand up to the bayonet charge of disciplined troops. But by the same reasoning the British from their own position could have expected to decimate an attack by less well-trained men across the bridge, even if supported by artillery. Wasting time on fortifications around Norfolk that he could not maintain, Dunmore neglected too long strengthening the post where a small force might have made a more successful stand.

Leslie had 120 regulars, about 60 loyalists, and some sailors from the fleet plus 100 men already at the fort. He relaid the planks on the bridge and quickly moved the attacking force across to the island, from which the rebel outposts withdrew after a few shots. According to local legend, the last to leave was a black man named William Flora. Leslie set up cannon on the island and left loyalist and black troops to guard them. Since scattered shots were commonplace the main body of Virginians was not immediately alarmed and went about the daily routine for several minutes before the cry went up, "Boys, stand to your arms." From the island Capt. Charles Fordyce led the regulars onto the causeway toward the Virginia barricade, which was defended by 70 or 80 men under Lt. Edward Travis. The latter held their fire until the British were almost upon them. The effect was devastating; a Virginian later wrote of "10 or 12 bullets thro' many; limbs broke in 2 or 3 places; brains turned out." Capt. Fordyce was killed and Lt. John Batut wounded just as they reached the barricade.

Falling back to the island the survivors commenced firing on Woodford's main force, which was marching down the street from its camp, but with ludicrous effect. The sole Virginia casualty in the entire engagement was a soldier nicked in the finger, an ironic

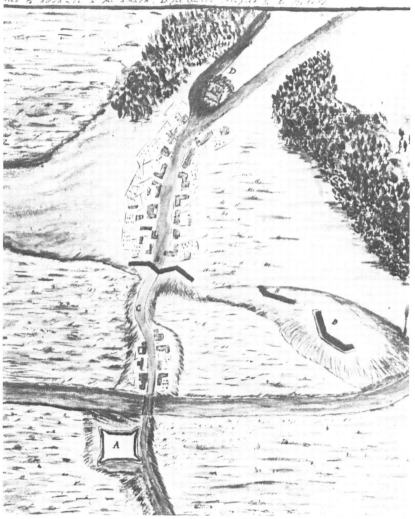

"A View of the Great Bridge near Norfolk in Virginia." *Courtesy of the W. L. Clements Library, Ann Arbor, Michigan.*

reversal of Kemp's Landing. Just then the Culpeper minutemen under Lt. Col. Stevens opened fire from the earthworks to the northeast, driving the British back into their fort. The battle lasted about thirty minutes, during which the 14th Regiment lost three officers including Leslie's nephew, Peter, and fourteen men killed, one officer and forty-eight wounded. Batut and fifteen other wounded were captured. The battle of Great Bridge, Woodford boasted, "was a second Bunker's Hill, in miniature, with this difference, that we kept our post."

To offset rumors that the shirtmen scalped their victims, Woodford made every effort to treat the British with perfect decorum. He buried the heroic Fordyce with full honors and was so solicitous toward Batut that the latter sent a message to Leslie assuring him of his good care. A truce was arranged to allow the British to take in their dead. Thirty-three blacks and tories, however, were handcuffed two by two and marched to Williamsburg for punishment.

Dunmore immediately realized that he could not hold Norfolk after the defeat. The British abandoned the "hogpen" that evening and, although some loyalists wanted to make another stand, moved their troops on board ship. Many residents had already provided vessels for themselves on which they crammed as much of their property as they could. Woodford occupied the fort the next day and was joined by a party of about 250 North Carolina regulars and militia under Col. Robert Howe, whose six cannon, however, turned out to be "honeycombed" and virtually useless. Two sound pieces arrived from Williamsburg a couple of days later.

Woodford was unable to move farther for several days because he had sent all his wagons back to Suffolk and Cabin Point in Surry County for supplies just before the battle. He also feared that a shipload of Highlanders reported off Norfolk might be British reinforcements, but a petition for safe conduct soon revealed them to be immigrants bound for the Carolinas. As stories of refugees exposed the extent of Dunmore's casualties, Woodford sent the Culpeper minutemen to Kemp's Landing on December 11, and after the arrival of another detachment of North Carolinians and several units from Williamsburg brought his strength to over 1,200, finally moved into Norfolk itself on the fourteenth. The next day the twenty-eight-gun *Liverpool* under Capt. Henry Bellew arrived with the storeship *Maria*, carrying 3,000 stand of arms. If only he had waited, Dunmore must have lamented.

For the rest of the month the British and Virginians eyed each other across the Norfolk waterfront. With hundreds packed on shipboard the British were in desperate need of fresh provisions which nearby farmers were willing to supply but which the rebels were just as determined to keep away. When a merchantman loaded with 4,000 bushels of salt, a commodity very scarce in Virginia and vital for preserving meat and fish, came within rifleshot the Virginians were able to force it to shore and beat off all rescue attempts. No bags could be found to unload it, however, and since the British controlled the water no one dared try to move it.

On the Hampton side a newly born Virginia navy fared better. While Patrick Henry was on a routine inspection of the defenses erected to prevent a repetition of the British raid the month before, two large, suspect merchant ships were sighted about fifteen miles out in Chesapeake Bay. Henry immediately commissioned a Hampton sea captain, James Barron, to man a small vessel with about twenty of his militia company to bring them in. Within ten days Barron and his brother Richard had nine other prizes waiting disposition by the Convention and had put an end to the freedom with which the British had been harassing Virginia shipping in Hampton Roads. The Convention voted its thanks to the Barrons and placed three armed vessels under James's command. It also reopened the admiralty court for the first time since the spring of 1774 in expectation of increasing business.

Although not as bad as on shipboard, life in Norfolk was not good, at least according to the steady stream of complaints directed to the Convention meeting in Williamsburg from the day the shirtmen entered the city. The weather was unbearable, the food abominable, and since there were so many ships to which suspicious trips could be made, the tours of duty too long. In sum, with its glory won, the 2nd Virginia Regiment felt it was time to go home and for someone else to endure the tedium of garrison duty.

Col. Howe, who had assumed command of the united forces by virtue of his Continental commission, reported a deluge of requests for leave or permission to resign, which under the circumstances he confessed that he and Woodford did not have the heart to deny. Discipline suffered, too, as men took sides over the way the Committee of Safety had treated Patrick Henry. One captain from Henry's command wrote back to his colonel, "We arrived there fatigued, dry & hungry, we were neither welcomed, invited to eat or drink, or shown a place to rest our weary bones." Openly defying Woodford, one lieutenant brought his men back from their post without permission on the ground that they were short of food, although they had ample flour and a half ration of meat. When Woodford had him court-martialed, he was acquitted. Woodford then appealed the verdict to the Convention, which turned him down. After that, the defendant took his case to the public in the pages of the *Virginia Gazette* and was answered in turn by a Woodford partisan.

As for Norfolk's future, the shirtmen were quite explicit. When frantic residents pleaded that their city be spared, Woodford and Howe issued a proclamation to assuage their immediate fears, but left the final decision to the Convention. Both commanders remained nervous over the possibility of a surprise landing if the British obtained reinforcements and initially asked the Convention for a massive increase in their own forces. Later they realized that even a large force could be cut off by the enemy at Portsmouth. Their recommendation and that of most of their officers was to abandon the city after making certain that it would be useless to the foe.

On Christmas eve, with the *Liverpool, Otter, King's Fisher, Dunmore,* and *William* riding abreast the town with springs on their anchor lines ready to fire, Capt. Bellew sent a message that he much preferred purchasing the fresh provisions he needed. Howe stalled by referring the request to the Convention (with a hint that they might agree since Bellew had been rather decent up to then) and raising the issue of a prisoner exchange, in which the British were very interested because of Lt. Batut. Dunmore offered to exchange rank for rank, but Howe refused unless the British recognized the American distinction between regulars, minutemen, and militia: "we can, by no means, submit to place the officers and soldiers of the army, who have been taken in battle, upon a footing with those officers of the militia and the peasants, that you have thought proper to deprive of their liberty." A little bewildered, Dunmore asked what that made a militia ensign (i.e., a second lieutenant) equal to, a noncommissioned officer in the regular service? He doubted that the militia would agree, and besides, all rebels were the same to him. He repeated his offer, at which point Howe broke off discussions and sent Batut to Williamsburg, where he was paroled.

Finally on December 30 Capt. Bellew ordered Howe to stop changing the guard in full view of his ships because it offended him as an officer of the crown to see rebels parading in public. Howe replied with stiff dignity that his men had orders not to fire first, but if Bellew insisted, would he please give women and children time to leave the city.

V

WHEN the Americans paraded again on New Year's Day, 1776, Bellew commenced firing between three and four o'clock in the afternoon. The cannonading continued steadily until about ten and intermittently into the morning. Although the British had no concerted plan to establish a beachhead, crews of individual ships that had been sniped at for days had favorite targets picked out for revenge. When Dunmore himself sent a boat to burn certain buildings and signaled Bellew to do the same to the captured shipload of salt, other vessels began sending parties ashore, a couple with field pieces, despite the efforts of their officers to restrain them. For most of the night the fighting and burning was general along the dock area.

On the American side, the first reaction of Woodford and Howe was that the attack was the major assault they feared. But once they saw that it was not, they had no objection to the British burning the town. "The wind favoured their design, and we believe the flames will become general," they hopefully reported only a few hours after the bombardment began. They had just requested permission from the Convention to burn the Thistle Distillery owned by Archibald Campbell and Neil Jamieson as well as Andrew Sprowle's establishment at Gosport across the Elizabeth River from Norfolk, from both of which the British had been obtaining supplies. Without waiting for an answer Woodford ordered these places destroyed as soon as the firing commenced. A counterattack by the British, however, prevented his men from reducing Robert Tucker's windmill near Portsmouth as well. The next morning, although the British had been repulsed, Woodford nonetheless informed the Committee of Safety that the fire had "now become general, and the whole town will, I doubt not, be consumed in a day or two."

For three days the Americans looted and burned their way through the city to the cry, "Keep up the Jigg." From Hampton a soldier described the view in a letter to his mother: "At night the fire was so great the Clouds above the Town appeared as red & bright as they do in an evening at sun setting." One witness testified later that the soldiers were "drinking Rum and were Crying out let us make hay while the Sun Shines;" another that Howe replied that he was too busy to interfere when the fires were reported to him.

James Parker's mansion, "with marble chimnies and stone steps" and "the best garden in that part of the country," was among the first to go. But tories were not the only ones to suffer. A witness related that Howe ordered him to stop bothering him when he complained about rebel properties being burned. Another told of shirtmen rekindling the blaze on Col. Joseph Hutchings's wharf when the wind repeatedly blew it out. John Calvert lost seven houses, and Thomas Newton nine tenements, ten warehouses, two "elegantly furnished" mansions, and a "well furnished" store. By the time Howe and Woodford finally restored order, Americans had destroyed 863 structures valued at a little under £120,000 in comparison with the British, who had burned 19 worth about £3,000. Earlier Dunmore had destroyed 32 houses valued at roughly £2,000 to build his fortifications.

Nothing of the truth was ever officially communicated to Williamsburg by Woodford or Howe, and amazing as it may be, there seems not even to have been a rumor. From the first news of the conflagration everyone automatically assumed Dunmore was the sole culprit. He was also said to be planning the destruction of Portsmouth and Yorktown. On January 13 Howe was in Williamsburg to report to the Convention and to be feted, but by all indications said nothing except to recommend that the rest of Norfolk be demolished. Reluctantly, the Convention and Committee of Safety approved the request "since that Town was set on fire by our enemies." Seemingly the first inkling of the truth that the Williamsburg authorities had was the story in Dunmore's *Gazette* on January 15. Two weeks later the Committee of Safety ordered Howe to investigate, but nothing more was heard until petitions from Norfolk authorities revived the investigation over a year later. At that time the damage done by the rebel troops was admitted and compensation provided for any sufferer who was not a tory. The official report, however, was not made public until sixty years later.

After the first fire there were three more skirmishes on January 20 and 21 and on February 1 when small detachments of British landed to burn three houses that snipers were still using and to take some tobacco. But eventually Howe completed the destruction of the remaining 416 structures and departed from the city on February 6. "We have removed from Norfolk, thank God for that!" he announced, "It is entirely destroyed; thank God for that also!" He left guards of about 300 men each at Kemp's Landing and Great Bridge as he withdrew to a new base camp at Suffolk.

The popular impression of what happened at Norfolk was of great importance in promoting acceptance of the idea of independence. When Sam Adams learned of the incident, he wrote to Joseph Warren of Massachusetts, "This will prevail more than a long train of Reasoning to accomplish a Confederation, and other Matters which I know your heart as well as mine is much set upon." Generally Norfolk was linked in men's minds with the burning of Falmouth, as Portland, Maine, was then called, two and a half months before. Together, said Washington in his camp outside Boston, they were "flaming arguments" that "will not leave numbers at a loss to decide upon . . . separation." In Virginia John Page could still write as, unknown to him, the bombardment of Norfolk was going on, "it is possible that matters may be accommodated in a short time." A month or so later he was ready to leave the empire.

Soon after Howe withdrew from Norfolk more help for Dunmore arrived. The forty-four-gun *Roebuck* under Capt. Andrew Snape Hamond with 100 marines entered Chesapeake Bay on February 9. Its presence ended the possibility that an attack upon Dunmore would be one of the first assignments for the newly formed Continental navy. About two months before Congress had ordered an expedition and had brought two pilots from the Chesapeake to Philadelphia to guide its fleet. Delays in the shipyard held up departure until early February. No sooner had the ships left Delaware Bay than Congress learned of the *Roebuck,* which with the *Liverpool* was too formidable to attack, and ordered the commander-in-chief, Esek Hopkins of Rhode Island, to sail for the Caribbean instead.

With Hamond's support Dunmore occupied Tucker's Point, a small promontory jutting into the Elizabeth River from the Portsmouth side. Although some of the buildings had been damaged during the Norfolk fire, the windmill remained standing, and

Dunmore proceeded to add ovens and wells to relieve the food and water shortage. Barracks were constructed to provide welcome respite from the overcrowding on shipboard and, with smallpox breaking out, a place to which to move the sick.

A week after Hamond arrived, Gen. Sir Henry Clinton put in to Chesapeake Bay on the *Mercury* accompanied by three transports and several tenders. On first sighting the incoming ships Dunmore naturally assumed that they were his long awaited reinforcements. To his "inexpressible mortification" he learned from Clinton that the fleet was actually on its way to meet Charles Lord Cornwallis coming with more troops from England for an attack on North Carolina. The expedition was in response to the chorus of southern governors who had been assuring the government in London that loyalists could easily restore royal authority in their provinces. Clinton was to strike quickly, establish the tories in power, and rejoin the new commander-in-chief, Gen. William Howe, in time for the main campaign of 1776 in the North. On the strength of Gov. Martin's reports and a talk with Gov. Tryon of New York, who was formerly in North Carolina, Clinton expected 5,000 or 6,000 tories to meet him in the latter colony, more even than Dunmore was promising, and lingered in Chesapeake Bay only until February 26 for repairs.

Upon learning the bad news, Dunmore immediately sat down at his desk to let London know what he thought of the plan. How the ministry could prefer "a most insignificant province" to "the first Colony of the Continent, both for Riches and Power" was beyond him. Virginia contained a perfect naval base from which to operate against the southern and middle colonies. "To see my Government thus totally neglected," he fulminated, "I own is a mortification I was not prepared to meet with after being imprisoned on board a Ship between eight or nine months and now left without a hope of relief either to myself or the many unhappy friends to Government that are now afloat suffering with me *but I have done*. [And in large, bristling characters] DUNMORE."

Clinton's expedition south coincided with the last flurry of rumors over possible reconciliation. In the king's speech to Parliament the previous fall and in the parliamentary act prohibiting colonial trade were references to the impending appointment of peace commissioners. At the same time there were private efforts in the North to explore the feasibility of renewed negotiations. Eventually Gen. Howe and his brother, Adm. Richard Lord Howe, were named commissioners. In this context Dunmore had written to the receiver-general, Richard Corbin, asking him to act as liaison with the Committee of Safety, and on February 22 the governor, Corbin, and Clinton met on board the *Roebuck*.

The setting was not auspicious. The day on which Corbin had presented Dunmore's letter to the Committee of Safety and requested permission to visit him, the committee was debating plans to call up more troops in response to the invasion shiver that Clinton's arrival sent through the colony. The committee granted Corbin a pass, but told him that it would have to leave all negotiations to Congress. It did offer to deliver Dunmore's message to the General Assembly if he ever let it meet again. In the meantime, it suggested, Dunmore could show his goodwill by ending hostilities and returning all the slaves he was harboring.

For his part, Dunmore admitted in his account to London that he just wanted to have the Virginians refuse to negotiate once more to prove his contention that they had been aiming at independence right along. Only Corbin seemed to have any hope that he might win even a momentary truce. Yet, although once among the staunchest of the governor's supporters and the man whom Dunmore had been instructed to leave as lieutenant governor should he decide to leave Virginia, Corbin let it be known that he planned to give Capt. Hamond "a true statement of Lord Dunmore's conduct."

On the way out to the *Roebuck* with a flag of truce, Corbin and his small escort of soldiers from Hampton were stopped by a half dozen of Dunmore's ships and made to come aboard each time for inspection. They were treated so discourteously by all but one that when they returned the escort commander, Maj. Leven Powell of Loudoun County, sent back to the hospitable crew twenty bushels of oysters, thirty loaves of bread, a goose, and a turkey in appreciation. On the *Roebuck*, however, Capt. Hamond treated the negotiating team to a royal breakfast with the best Hyson tea. Otherwise, Clinton merely observed of the Committee of Safety's reply that Parliament would never accept Congress as a constitutional body, while Dunmore rejected Corbin's suggestion that he delegate authority to Thomas Nelson, president of the Council, to call the General Assembly if he did not want to come ashore to do so himself. Instead, Dunmore offered to take one more petition from the Virginians back to Great Britain when he returned.

Meanwhile the Committee of Safety and the Convention were

accelerating their military efforts. The Convention authorized recruitment of seven more regiments in order to station two on each of the Tidewater peninsulas and one on the Eastern Shore. As six were to be placed on the Continental payroll, there was a fair flurry of excitement when Congress first decided not to include the original 1st and 2nd Regiments because their year's enlistment was half over. When that question was settled to the Virginians' liking, a greater crisis loomed: Congress bypassed Patrick Henry to name the old Indian fighter, Andrew Lewis, brigadier general. Henry immediately resigned and then had to spend the whole night going among the troops of his regiment who were camped around Williamsburg to keep them from mutiny in protest.

It was into this situation of unrest that Maj. Gen. Charles Lee arrived on March 29. A native Englishman, Lee was a soldier of fortune who had seen service in the British, Polish, and Russian armies and whom Congress at the moment deemed its most promising military talent. At the news of Clinton's expedition to the South, Continental authorities dispatched him to assume overall command of the defense. Because he could not be certain whether Clinton would double back to attack Virginia or go on to strike at North or South Carolina, Lee decided to remain in Williamsburg; from there he could move quickly in whatever direction he was needed. While there, he occupied his time by trying to teach the Virginia troops some discipline and to instill energy in their leaders, whom he considered hopelessly inept. "From Pendleton, Bland, the Treasurer & Company, libera nos Domine," he wrote to the North.

Lee was particularly irate over the lack of action against tories and Dunmore. The Committee of Safety had been lenient toward loyalists not actually taken under arms, most of whom it acquitted or paroled. Others like Col. Ellegood were rusticated to counties far enough to the west to minimize the possibility of their rejoining Dunmore. Only a few, like the Goodriches, were closely confined. Against Dunmore, who had remained relatively quiet since he moved to Tucker's Point, virtually nothing had been done. Lee immediately ordered most of the new regiments to concentrate around Williamsburg since the way they had been scattered around the colony rendered offense virtually impossible. He called a council of war to approve driving out all inhabitants on the Norfolk side of Great Bridge in order to eliminate the governor's main source of food.

Lee almost had his way when shortly after his arrival a Virginia

53

cruiser captured dispatches from London to Gov. Robert Eden of Maryland. Until then Eden had succeeded in building an image contrasting sharply with Dunmore's by following a relatively conciliatory policy in order to divide the opposition. The dispatches now revealed that from the American point of view, Eden was as bad as the Virginia governor, only quieter. He, too, had recommended the use of force. The communications also afforded the first solid evidence the colonists had of a large fleet coming from England for the invasion of the Carolinas "or Virginia." The captured documents "had a good effect here," John Page reported to Richard Henry Lee in Philadelphia, "I think almost every man, except the Treasurer, is willing to declare for independence."

Alarmed at the renewed prospect of invasion, the Committee of Safety finally cracked down on tories. Lee was authorized to arrest Ralph Wormeley, Jr., of Middlesex County, whose letter promising to join Dunmore as soon as the loyalist cause did not seem so "useless" had been intercepted, along with another compromising letter to John Agnew, the tory rector of Suffolk. Lee ordered Woodford to begin removing people from the dangerous area around Norfolk and, going to assess the situation in Portsmouth himself, had the homes of the Goodriches, Andrew Sprowle, Neil Jamieson, and others razed. Commanding the remaining residents to be prepared for evacuation within five days, he returned to Williamsburg with the recommendation that the whole town be burned since the people were "universally" tory.

When no invasion materialized by the end of April, the committee began to relent, especially after its chairman, Edmund Pendleton, who had slipped away for a well-earned vacation at his home in Caroline County soon after Lee took charge, returned to urge moderation. Wormeley and Agnew were acquitted, and the evacuation of Princess Anne County was temporarily stayed until tories could be sorted out from those sympathetic to the rebels' cause. Lee immediately appealed to the Convention the decision to delay the evacuation, and the Convention rescinded it. But by then Woodford reported that he could not find enough wagons to move the 20,000 people he estimated were involved.

Nonetheless, Lee did succeed in stimulating the campaign against Dunmore. He imposed severe discipline on the troops; according to one report, he "flogged them in scores." His engineers, John Stadler and a German named Massenbach, aided by a French artillery expert,

Dohicky Arundel, repaired the dilapidated fortifications at Yorktown, Jamestown, and Hampton and drilled a company of gunners in the use of cannon. Lee continued his centralization of the Virginia forces by collecting all the weapons he could for the regular troops rather than leaving them in the hands of the militia, and he opened enlistments for a cavalry troop. One of his favorite schemes was to arm two companies of the tallest men in each regiment with thirteen-foot spears in the fashion of Roman legions. "It has a fine effect to the eye, and the men in general seemed convinced of the utility of the arrangement," he reported to Philadelphia. Lee's dynamism antagonized many. Local interests objected to being left unprotected when troops moved to the capital, and the Committee of Safety sharply reminded him that civil authorities must always control the military in a free society. That reprimand came when he took over the Palace for his own use and converted the College of William and Mary into a hospital without asking permission.

Lee's survey of Portsmouth also convinced him that an attack against Dunmore on Tucker's Point under the guns of the British fleet would be hazardous without naval support. The Convention had previously authorized the construction of eight row galleys, two for each of the principal Tidewater rivers. These were shallow draft vessels propelled by oars and sails, carrying about forty men each and a variety of weapons. They proved effective darting out from the mouths of small streams to fire at passing British ships and quickly retreating. Two of these, the *Norfolk Revenge* commanded by John Calvert and the *Hero* commanded by George Muter, were well along in construction, and Lee urged the builders, Archibald Cary and John Herbert, to greater efforts. The final campaign against Dunmore awaited their completion. Meanwhile, Lee ordered the preparation of fire rafts upstream on the Elizabeth River to float down into the midst of Dunmore's squadron. About that time, however, he learned that Clinton was in the Cape Fear region. He set out for North Carolina from Williamsburg on May 13, leaving the Committee of Safety to deal with the governor.

Events moved quickly in the next few days. The fifth Virginia Convention had assembled in Williamsburg on May 6. Before it met, a few delegates who were members of the last House of Burgesses gathered in the Capitol to "neither proceed to Business, nor adjourn, as a House of Burgesses." The desire for independence in Virginia had advanced rapidly during March and April although a few like

55

Edmund Pendleton and Robert Carter Nicholas remained hesitant. Encouragement also came from Philadelphia, where advocates were having difficulty overcoming the reluctance of the middle colonies. A decision by Virginia would have great effect.

It came on May 15 when after extended debate the Convention adopted the famous Virginia Resolution for Independence. Although North Carolina had already granted permission to its congressional delegates to join in any vote for separation from the empire, the Virginia resolution was the first to direct a colony's representatives to move a public declaration of independence. In the final compromise version of the resolution, written by Edmund Pendleton, the delegates were obviously greatly concerned to give one last reply to Dunmore's charges that they had been seeking independence from the beginning. The fault belonged entirely to Great Britain they said; the king had put them out of his protection and his governor had waged "a piratical and savage war against us." They called upon "the Searcher of Hearts" to witness "the sincerity of former declarations expressing our desire to preserve the connection with that nation, and that we are driven from that inclination by their wicked councils, and the eternal law of self-preservation."

The Convention immediately appointed a committee to prepare a Declaration of Rights and a constitution for the new state, but in the midst of its deliberations Dunmore suddenly abandoned his base at Tucker's Point. Spies following the progress of the fireships that Lee had commissioned had reported that at last they were ready. The rebel plan was to follow them downstream and attempt to board as many of Dunmore's vessels as possible. One spy who had crept into a house and pretended to be asleep while Maj. Thomas Parker and the other officers in charge were conversing related that, when asked what to do about the tories with Dunmore, Parker replied, "Damn them, Tomahawk them all and throw them over Board, and give yourself no further trouble about them."

Dunmore sent for aid to Hamond, who had been patroling Delaware Bay for the past month and was at that moment bound to join Sir Peter Parker's fleet off South Carolina. Fortunately for Dunmore, Hamond was just off the Virginia capes when he received the message and reached Hampton Roads quickly to recommend immediate evacuation of Tucker's Point before the rebels could place cannon downstream to trap Dunmore's ships. Without Hamond, Dunmore would have been in trouble, for the navy had to supply crews for many of the ninety-odd private vessels that had no one on board who knew how to sail. Even so, Hamond had to scuttle three or four ships "for want of materials to navigate." It took three days to demolish the buildings at Tucker's Point and collect the fleet at the mouth of the Elizabeth River. Then, sailing as if to pass through the capes, the British suddenly turned up the Chesapeake Bay and "with more trouble and difficulty than ever I had before experienced," Hamond said, reached Gwynn's Island at the mouth of the Piankatank River on May 27.

Unquestionably Dunmore and Hamond could have found a safer place to go. At the nearest point the island was only 200 yards from the mainland across a channel that could be forded at low tide. Smallpox had left only 150 to 200 effective troops to defend its three or four square miles, and Hamond had to lend some of his sailors to throw up entrenchments. He and Dunmore picked the site largely on the recommendation of John Randolph Grymes, who owned land there and who was given the task of equipping a cavalry troop with horses from the island. Grymes reported it "to be inhabited by many Friends of Government, that it formed an excellent Harbour, had plenty of fresh water on it, and could easily be defended from the Enemy." It did contain 300 to 400 head of cattle that eased the food shortage, but a mid-summer dry spell soon reduced the water supply. Yet Hamond could describe it to his superiors as "the best rendezvous of any in Virginia for the fleet," and Dunmore set his men to constructing a windmill and other structures useful for a base of operations.

Hamond and Dunmore still had in mind the possibility that Clinton would stop to help on the way back from the southern campaign. Off the North Carolina coast, Clinton, who had discretion over the actual point of invasion, remained undecided where to go. The original plan, which depended upon the synchronization of his movements with those of the Scottish tories of the Cape Fear River Valley and Lord Cornwallis coming from England, had completely fallen through. On February 27, just two weeks after Cornwallis had sailed from Cork, Ireland, the impatient North Carolina loyalists challenged the rebels at Moore's Creek Bridge and suffered so devastating a defeat that a landing in the Cape Fear area was senseless. Storms delayed Cornwallis until early May, raising the question whether there was time for Clinton to accomplish his objectives without violating his instruction to rejoin the main British army under Gen.

Howe at New York for its summer campaign. A return to Virginia might be the only course remaining.

Hamond and Dunmore were also counting heavily on being in a better position in their new post to tap the reservoir of loyalist activity on the Eastern Shore and the Chesapeake Bay islands. Dunmore had been in contact with Eastern Shore leaders off and on all winter and reestablished communications through "a mysterious gentleman in black." He was especially confident that the recent resolution for independence would generate an upswell of sentiment for the king. In a month's time a couple of hundred recruits were obtained for the Queen's Own Loyal Regiment although in the same period as many already in ranks were lost to the pox. H. M. S. *Fowey* was able to bring off Gov. Eden from Annapolis, where the local Committee of Safety granted his request for a safe conduct to leave, though at the last minute Eden had to go without his baggage because the *Fowey's* captain refused to return some indentured servants who fled with him.

The sudden move to Gwynn's Island caught Virginia leaders completely by surprise. "I never heard of such a Place before the Enemy reached it," confessed Andrew Lewis. Coming at the same time as Eden's request for safe passage, the arrival of a captured transport with 217 Scottish Highland troops originally destined for Boston, and news that the American invasion of Canada over the past winter had collapsed because of reinforcements arriving from England, the new development sent another round of invasion nerves through Virginia. It seemed that a concerted attempt by the mother country to end the rebellion quickly was under way. Hesitating to commit too many troops at Gwynn's lest Dunmore was trying to lure him from the Williamsburg area, Lewis sent Col. William Daingerfield from Gloucester County and Col. Hugh Mercer from Fredericksburg to pin him down. But again, because the rebels were without cannon, the British easily checked them at the water's edge.

The standoff at least let the Convention go back to work designing its new government. On June 12 it adopted the Declaration of Rights, the first such statement in America, which became a model for similar assertions of basic individual liberties by other states, the federal Bill of Rights, and the Declaration of the Rights of Man and of the Citizen during the French Revolution. Then, on June 29, the Convention enacted a new constitution that reflected the deep distrust of executive power ingrained in Virginians by their knowledge of past struggles of the English with their kings and their own experience with Dunmore and his predecessors.

Under the new constitution, the governor, now to be elected by a joint ballot of the two houses of the legislature, was limited to three successive terms of one year each, after which he had to wait four years before he could serve again. Moreover, the constitution virtually established a plural executive by requiring the governor to act in most matters on the advice of an eight-man Council, which was elected for staggered terms by joint ballot of the legislature. The Council, too, which under royal government had tended to side with the governor, was no longer both the upper house of the legislature and the principal court of the province, as well as part of the executive branch. A separate Senate and an independent judiciary were created instead. The governor was shorn of the power enjoyed by his royalist predecessors of adjourning or dissolving the legislature. He could call it into session but could not send it home; nor could he veto its acts. Finally, having established the new government on this basis, the Convention elected Patrick Henry the first governor of the Commonwealth of Virginia and disbanded. Henry, although acutely ill at the time, was inaugurated on July 6, two days after the signing in Congress of the Declaration of Independence.

On July 8 Gen. Andrew Lewis marched from Williamsburg for Gwynn's Island with units of the veteran 1st and 2nd Regiments. In the intervening weeks he had resolved his manpower problems by calling up 1,300 militiamen and obtaining the release of two battalions held in reserve for Maj. Gen. Lee. When Lewis reached the camp opposite Gwynn's Island, he found that the British had several hundred men bivouacked in tents at the western end of the island and an artillery battery strengthened by James Parker through three days and sleepless nights at the place where the channel was narrowest. Stationed in the channel near that point were the *Otter* and several tenders, ready to thwart the expected onslaught. On the Virginian side, the French artillery director, Dohicky Arundel, had brought every piece that could be spared from posts around the Tidewater to assemble a battery of impressive firepower: two eighteen-pounders, two twelve-pounders, five nine-pounders, three six-pounders, and two field pieces. All that remained was for the shirtmen to collect enough rowboats, canoes, and rafts from around the neighborhood for an amphibious assault.

The next morning, however, Lewis noticed that the *Dunmore* had

59

changed positions with the *Otter* and was exposed to the two eighteen-pounders which the Virginians had been able to mount unobserved. Without waiting to find more boats, Lewis ordered the gunners to open fire at eight o'clock. Taken unaware, the British had no weapon in place large enough to reply. The *Dunmore* was hit a dozen times, the governor himself slightly wounded, and the ship's mate killed before the vessel could be towed out of range. It was saved primarily by the fact that the skirmish occurred at ebb tide. When the *Otter* came to the rescue, it was seriously damaged, and four tenders in the channel were driven aground, three to be burned and one captured. Two more were burned the next day along with a larger ship, the *Logan*. James Parker's battery, in which the largest weapon was a six-pounder, was silenced after a little over an hour.

What saved Dunmore was the Virginians' lack of boats. He had about forty-eight hours to flee before they could reach the island. Having learned that Clinton had finally made up his mind to attack Charleston, South Carolina, thus ending any possibility of his coming to Virginia in the immediate future, and realizing that his own troops were too weak from smallpox to make a stand, Dunmore ordered their withdrawal that night.

There was consternation among the Norfolk refugees, for despite frequent warnings from the military to be ready to move on a moment's notice, many had neglected to store fresh water on board. Others had to leave much valuable gear behind in their scramble. Once again, the navy was forced to furnish crews. About thirty blacks too ill to move were all that remained when the Virginians came ashore. The one casualty on their side was Dohicky Arundel, who, in his professional enthusiasm, insisted against all advice on firing a wooden mortar with which he was experimenting and was killed.

Once off Gwynn's Island, Dunmore and Hamond were ready to leave Virginia as soon as they had obtained a supply of fresh water. In search of it they headed up Chesapeake Bay to St. George's Island at the mouth of the Potomac River, where they temporarily landed troops to hold off Maryland militia on the mainland. Finding little fresh water there, Dunmore took a few of the warships and some detachments of the 14th and Queen's Own Loyal Regiments to forage a hundred miles or so upriver until they had a supply for the entire fleet. At George Brent's plantation near Dumfries, local militia foolishly dared them to land and, when they did, hid in the woods, where the approach of their own reinforcements so frightened them

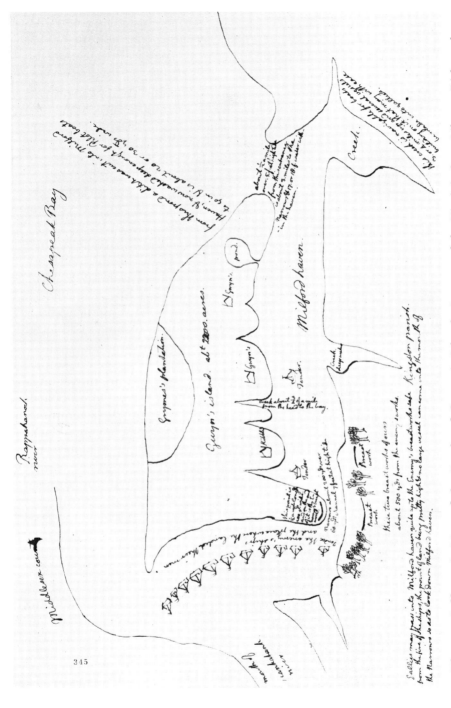

Thomas Jefferson's Map of the Battle of Gwynn's Island. *Courtesy of the Virginia State Library, Richmond.*

61

that they ran themselves "almost to death." In retaliation for the resistance, Dunmore burned Brent's house and was about to do the same to Hugh Mercer's when a change in the wind forced him to return to the main flotilla.

After loading their casks of water, Dunmore and Hamond scuttled about twenty vessels that were unfit for sea. Overall losses were heavy. "A violent bilious intermitting fever, together with a most inveterate scurvy had for these two months past raged with great violence both in the men of war and Transports," Hamond reported. His own *Roebuck* lost thirty seamen. Dunmore's army had left about 300 graves at Tucker's Point and about half that number on Gwynn's Island. Then, on August 4, Dunmore and Hamond learned that, having failed to invest Charleston, Clinton was sailing back to New York. Three days later the governor's flotilla passed through the Virginia capes. About fifty vessels followed the *Otter* to St. Augustine, Florida, a handful went with Gov. Eden to England, and the rest turned northward with Dunmore for New York, where they arrived on August 13. The following day, Dunmore attended "a great formal Dinner" to tell his story to Gen. Howe and others of the British high command.

The Virginians had driven Dunmore out just in time. His departure coincided with the first call for Virginia regiments to march north. While he was still at sea on the way to New York, the 1st and 3rd Regiments set out from Williamsburg to join Washington's army on Long Island, and five more followed in succeeding months. With the one-year enlistments of many Continental veterans running out, the Virginians provided new strength against the 25,000-man army that the British were amassing under Howe. The fear verging on panic that affected many in the Virginia government in the autumn of 1776 as unit after unit of the colony's best troops marched away— Patrick Henry even proposed a temporary dictatorship—suggests the difficulties that Dunmore might have caused. As a tactician he proved inept at Great Bridge, but as a strategist he was sound. Had British commanders been less cautious, or had they more forces at their disposal, a few ships and a few hundred troops in Virginia early in the war might have generated a more serious "tory problem" or forced diversion that would have weakened the American war effort.

VI

Virginia had not heard the last of Lord Dunmore, although he never again stepped on Virginia soil. For a long while his name alone was enough to revive invasion jitters. Dunmore was a bitter man. He departed with a firm resolution to come back to prove that he was right, a resolution he relentlessly pursued during the entire course of the war. He never yielded his belief that most Virginians, especially in the West, were loyal and that the failure of his administration was because his superiors had not adequately supported him. He remained in New York through the early fall of 1776, dining frequently with Gen. Howe and his officers and insistently dunning them for troops with which to return and conquer Virginia. As late as November the *Virginia Gazette* ran a story that from his headquarters on Broadway he was preparing to set out with a 10,000-man army. But Howe's energies at the time were consumed chasing Washington around New York. Finally, on November 12, Dunmore gave up his quest for the time being and sailed on H.M.S. *Fowey* for home.

There he awaited his chance for five years. He reentered politics as a representative peer in the House of Lords, from which Lord North had dropped him a couple of years before because he could not attend, although with assurances that he could have the first vacancy upon his return. Coming back must have been hard, for he was the butt of opposition jokes aimed at the government's mishandling of the war. At one reference to royal forces making a stand, Edmund Burke retorted, "Where was that? On board Lord Dunmore's ship?" and later wisecracked, "Neptune they say is to have a pension Like Lord Dunmore for having lost his government." The optimism of Dunmore's earlier reports had made good copy for the British press, and now his bragging returned to haunt him.

To his credit, Dunmore was loyal to those who had fought for him. He prevailed upon Lord George Germain, who succeeded Lord Dartmouth as secretary of state for the colonies, to intercede personally with Gen. Howe to expedite the exchange of loyalist captives, such as James Parker and the Goodrich family. In those particular cases, however, the Americans did not cooperate. In time, Dunmore emerged as a leader of the loyalist lobby in London, arguing the tories' cause before various governmental agencies. He himself was involved in a long bureaucratic wrangle over his right to "bat and forage," or living allowances, during the Virginia campaign. Only officers ordered into the field by the king were eligible, and the issue was whether the king's subsequent approbation of Dunmore's taking up arms sufficed. Dunmore also had trouble producing adequate vouchers for his expenditures during his campaign, and five years after his flight there were still questions about his salary for his last year in Virginia. But in general he was well treated. In 1777 Lord North allowed him £15,000 toward final settlement of his losses and permitted him to draw his £2,000 annual salary, plus £1,000 a year supplemental compensation, throughout the war.

Late in 1777 Dunmore proposed that he be allowed to recruit 4,000 men among the Scottish clans to form a regiment under his command as colonel. But the clans he suggested already had been committed to raise other units, and in addition, the king objected that Dunmore would have to be jumped several grades to be given command since he had not been in active service for almost twenty years and was still only a captain.

Finally, the focus of British strategy in America shifted from the northern colonies, and in 1780 Gen. Charles Earl Cornwallis was sent with a major expeditionary force into the South. In April of the next year, as Cornwallis marched into Virginia, Dunmore at last received permission to raise whatever forces he needed to resume control of civil government in the colony. The order was symptomatic of the ministry's inability to learn. The idea of sending Dunmore to pacify a people who detested him struck even some British advisers as incredible. For his main corps all Virginia tories who were receiving allowances from the British government were commanded to accompany him or forfeit their pensions. The order was rigorously enforced, regardless of excuse, and on his roster appeared the names of many, such as John Randolph Grymes, James Ingram, and John Brown, who had served him before. Even widows who were still receiving their husband's payments were instructed to go, until Lord Germain intervened on the ground that they "could not be of the least use in Virginia."

Dunmore received strong support from Germain, who was willing to act on assurances that the former governor still commanded a following in the Virginia backcountry, although he was beginning to have some private doubts. Letters from the secretary opened royal armories to Dunmore, who busied himself through the spring and summer collecting the arms he would need. Among other items, he obtained twelve thirty-two-pound cannon and was permitted to order six sixty-eight-pounders cast to his specifications. He was not going to be caught short again! All except the sixty-eight-pounders were ready for loading aboard the transports *Laurie* and *Juliana* in September, and early the next month Dunmore was on his way back to America.

Dunmore reached Charleston, South Carolina, on December 21, 1781, to learn of Cornwallis's surrender at Yorktown two months before. Still he did not give up. All winter he planned, each scheme becoming more grandiose. He wrote to Lord Germain proposing that he be allowed to raise a force of tories entirely separate from the regular military establishment—an arrangement that would have avoided the question both of his own and others' rank and the increasing desire of many British regulars to be out of America—with which he was confident he could subdue the southern colonies. When the proposal was shown to the king, Germain wrote, the monarch brushed it aside with the remark that Dunmore should "make known . . . every particular respecting the situation and Circumstances of *your lordship*'s Government" to the commander-in-chief in America.

In the same letter, however, Dunmore set forth the outlines of a more ambitious scheme suggested to him by a South Carolina tory, John Cruden. Observing the number of ex-slaves fleeing to the British lines at Charleston, Cruden proposed recruiting an army of 10,000 blacks with promises of freedom at the end of the war. Not just the able-bodied would be enlisted, for there were plans to have those who could not fight raise food and procure supplies for the others. Loyalists who allowed their slaves to join would be compensated.

Charleston at that moment was rife with such plans. Loyalists everywhere were appalled at Cornwallis's defeat and, panic-stricken, intensified pressure on British authorities not to abandon the war. The streams of British sympathizers filing into Charleston made it a

65

center of this sentiment. The British commanders, Lt. Gen. Alexander Leslie and Lt. Col. James Moncrief, themselves wrote to Clinton wondering whether the war was to go on and indicating that, if it was, the recruitment of blacks was absolutely necessary. Whether Dunmore was at the center of such thinking or merely a participant is not clear, but the activity at Charleston was enough for the French commander, comte de Rochambeau, wintering with his victorious army at Williamsburg, to be disturbed by rumors that Dunmore was preparing to invade Virginia again. In April Dunmore was in New York, reporting that Lt. Col. Moncrief, in charge of the engineers at Charleston, was ready to establish a post at either Old Point Comfort or Sewell's Point. Clinton responded that he was quite willing to consider the move, although he added, "the arming of negroes requires a little consideration. I will, as soon as possible, let you know my ideas."

By then Dunmore had a still grander vision—one that was to influence the rest of his career. Robert Ross, a British merchant long resident at Natchez and New Orleans and an associate of David Ross, a merchant in Richmond, presented Dunmore a long manuscript pointing out the advantage to Great Britain of shifting attention to Louisiana and the Mississippi Valley. Not only did the Mississippi River offer communication to Canada and the lands of the Ohio Valley, into which settlers were already moving, but it could open to British exploitation the trans-Mississippi West and the silver mines of Mexico. To cap his proposal, Ross provided an intricate description of New Orleans defenses and a detailed plan of attack. Dunmore was only the first of the contacts Ross made in lobbying for his scheme, for it reached the British high command by other channels, too.

April 1782, however, was no time for such dreams. Dunmore reached New York in the last weeks of Clinton's tenure as commander-in-chief. Sir Guy Carleton shortly arrived with instructions to wind down the war with as much grace as possible. Already in the various capitals peace feelers were out. Clinton's final days, moreover, were marred by a bitter confrontation with the loyalist forces in New York, who had taken an American prisoner out to Long Island on the pretext of exchanging him and hanged him instead. The only hope for loyalists, it seemed, was back in London, where by June Dunmore was pressing upon the ministry a revised combination of his earlier plans. Let loyalists who wanted to do so seek a new home on the Mississippi, and, if the British army had no stomach for continuing the war, let loyalists carry it on under a separate command.

Dunmore soon came forth as a major spokesman for the loyalist campaign to obtain compensation from the British government and found himself plunged into London politics. Having lost the war, Lord North had been replaced in March by the principal critic of his American policy, the marquis of Rockingham. Then, upon the latter's sudden death in July, the mantle fell to the earl of Shelburne, Dunmore's old friend, with whom, however, he had had little contact for almost twenty years. In negotiating an American peace, Shelburne ignored loyalist petitions for allowances for fear of conceding that his treaty did not protect British interests as well as it might. With Joseph Galloway of Pennsylvania and the ex-governor of Maryland, Robert Eden, among others, Dunmore organized a lobbying effort in Parliament that embarrassed Shelburne and contributed to his downfall in February 1783.

Dunmore eventually broke with the next ministry, too, although under it the loyalists first won important gains. Once more Lord North was secretary of state, but this time, surprisingly, in coalition with Charles James Fox, who had earned his reputation as an orator attacking North during the war. In July 1783, the government finally established a loyalist claims commission, and in the fall hearings began. Throughout the year Dunmore remained busy with other loyalist leaders working to insure the best possible presentation of cases and to expedite the frustratingly slow and cumbersome proceedings.

Just before Christmas Dunmore was summoned to London from his estates in Scotland by the duke of Portland, a supporter of the ministry, to vote for Fox's India bill. This bill proposed to reform the bankrupt East India Company, which, although a private corporation, was the agency through which Britain governed its possessions on the Indian subcontinent. Although almost everyone agreed that the company needed reform, the bill became controversial and a test of the ministry's strength. In particular, opponents observed that, while the bill purported to insulate the company's vast patronage from the "influence of the crown," as the public demanded, the ministry was substituting its favorites instead.

Many long-standing supporters of Lord North seized the opportunity to desert the coalition with Fox, whom they never liked. Dunmore joined them, declaring the bill "quite repugnant to my principles." Some of the deserters were defenders of Warren Hastings, the governor-general of Bengal, who bore the brunt of criticism of the company and whom the ministry was about to impeach for alleged misdeeds. Whether Dunmore was a friend of Hastings before that time is not known, but he became politically close to him during the subsequent trial. Probably most important, Dunmore's brother-in-law, Earl Gower, was one who shifted allegiance from Lord North to a political newcomer, the twenty-four-year-old son and namesake of William Pitt. When the India bill passed the House of Commons, the king, who earlier had appointed Fox to the cabinet only because there was no alternative, now advised the Lords "that he would consider all who voted for it as his enemies." Dunmore willingly complied, helping to assure Pitt's accession and Gower's return to the cabinet, but in the process earning the lasting enmity of the ousted ministerial faction, the duke of Portland in particular.

On February 25, 1784, Dunmore filed his own petition for compensation before the loyalist claims commission. His case was heard on July 9 and 10 and decided on July 23, although for some reason at least one witness was recalled in 1788. Dunmore asked for £32,723.16, covering the furnishings of the Governor's Palace in Williamsburg, a house and lot in that city, his country home Porto Bello in York County, his farm in Berkeley County (in modern West Virginia), 3,465 acres of lands rented out to tenants in Hampshire County (also in present West Virginia), 51,000 acres on Otter Creek on the eastern shore of Lake Champlain in modern Vermont, and 3,700,000 acres representing his share of the Illinois-Wabash Company's claim on the Wabash River in modern Indiana. In addition, he claimed compensation for cattle, horses, sheep, hogs, carriages, supplies of various sorts, a grist mill, a sawmill, 12 indentured servants, and 57 slaves. The commission granted him the full claim minus the £15,000 he had already received. The one item they disallowed was that for the Indiana lands, but Dunmore apparently expected that, as he had placed no cash value on them to be computed into the total. Essentially Dunmore lost only his reputation in Virginia.

VII

A youthful fifty-four when his claim was settled, Dunmore was ready for further employment and adventure. His political star was rising because his brother-in-law's was. In 1786 Lord Gower was created marquis of Stafford, and the same year a vacancy occurred in the governorship of the Bahama Islands. The post appealed to Dunmore. The population of the islands had more than doubled since the war with a great influx of American loyalists, principally from South Carolina, Georgia, and Florida. The British commander-in-chief at the end of the war, Gen. Carleton, had encouraged the migration and persuaded the crown to buy out the descendants of the original proprietors to provide lands for the newcomers. Most important, the Bahamas had become a base from which to fulfill loyalist dreams of reestablishing the empire in the American South and West. John Cruden was there, for example, and before Dunmore left London, he met and formed a partnership with a Floridian exile, John Miller, who said he knew in detail how to go about it. Dunmore's appointment was secured. After what was by now a typical delay, he arrived at his post in October of the following year.

The pattern of Dunmore's third administration was much the same as that of the earlier two and serves to place them in perspective. His style was as freewheeling and pugnacious. There were the same displays of temper. Once he allegedly caned a man in the street "without the slightest provocation"—at least according to the victim. His concern for his family extended now to nepotism when he appointed his son, Alexander, collector of customs for Turks Island and then tried to name him lieutenant governor. He lived in the same grand manner: expanding and redecorating Government House, building a summer home called the Hermitage, and holding gala

69

celebrations, such as one for George III at which "an elegant entertainment was given at the Government-House and in the evening there was the most splendid illumination ever seen."

The lack of proportion that Dunmore revealed at Norfolk led in Nassau to a raging controversy over building grandiose fortifications that once again he did not have enough troops to man. That cost virtually bankrupted the colony, and the expenditures generated charges of corruption. He clashed with the legislature over whether they had any voice in the matter and whether there was a constitutional requirement that he hold general elections at least every seventh year as in Great Britain. On both questions, the legislature passed resolves protesting that he treated it with "disrespect." Yet on both issues his position was once more identical to London's, where the American Revolution had not lessened concern over any apparent weakening of "prerogative" in the colonies. Most interesting, Dunmore's Bahamian administration revealed what a buccaneer he really was at heart. On at least two occasions he did not blink at private war to achieve his ends, just as before in Virginia.

In the Bahamas, Dunmore worked less well with the legislature from the start, probably because of conditions he inherited. He arrived in the midst of a major crisis between older inhabitants of the islands and loyalist newcomers. His predecessor had been driven into retirement because in the election of 1785 representation had not been extended to new arrivals as fully as they desired. It was expected that as a new governor Dunmore would hold another election that would remedy the situation, but London had sent instructions against too frequent elections, and Dunmore's own opinion of the practice had not changed. He waited eight more years.

Other issues, however, found recent immigrants on either side. Philip Dumaresq, a former Boston merchant whom Carleton had commissioned to lead one of the first groups of loyalists to the islands, became receiver general and the storm center of Dunmore's exorbitant building program. When Dunmore arrived, the islands' defenses had been in disrepair. Several times during the war, Americans had raided the islands because they were a threat to West Indian supply lines, and Spanish forces from Cuba had occupied them during the last year of the fighting. Consequently, Dunmore set about constructing the impregnable Fort Charlotte, armed with forty-two cannon, to guard Nassau on New Providence Island. He repeatedly expanded it and built fortifications on other islands as well. Then, to top his program, he erected a second fort at Nassau. No one gainsaid the need for new defenses, and undoubtedly the approach of the French Revolution encouraged precautions. But the expansion of a program originally budgeted at £4,000 to over £32,000 seriously strained the islands' economy. In addition, the legislature accused Dumaresq of embezzling funds, yet Dunmore refused to let them see the accounts on the ground that they could only appropriate money and had no right to determine or oversee its use. When the assembly appealed to London, they were told that there were other ways of dealing with Dumaresq without infringing upon executive authority.

As usual, Dunmore also plunged into the most promising speculative schemes of the moment. He managed to register for many of the lots that the government made available to loyalists when it bought out the proprietors, and he laid out the Bahamas' first housing subdevelopment, Dunmore Town.

But the real potential for speculation in the colony was in trade. At frequent intervals throughout his term the *Bahama Gazette* carried advertisements for cargoes imported from Great Britain on the ship *Dunmore*. The market for the imports was in Cuba, Florida, and Louisiana. For two decades the British had been experimenting with "free ports" in the Caribbean, hoping to legitimatize and capitalize on the widespread smuggling of the region by allowing foreigners to exchange raw materials for British manufactures in a few selected places, as the Dutch had been doing for so long and so profitably at St. Eustatius and Curaçao. Before he left London, Dunmore had seen to it that New Providence Island was added to the list.

In addition, there was smuggling to the United States. Although Americans were excluded from the free ports because Britain's direct trade in manufactures to the United States would suffer and the Americans were competitors for the West Indian trade in raw materials, most island colonies had long been dependent for foodstuffs upon the mainland. Immediately after the American war, there were riots in Nassau when embittered loyalists tried to pull down the colors of American ships bringing in food, and the government had to take suppressive measures. Dunmore continued the encouragement. One of the few memorials presented to him at his departure was from the residents of Crooked Island, the nearest of the Bahamas to the mainland, thanking him for "opening up these islands to American produce which alone prevented calamity." A few years later, incidentally, Crooked Island attained free port status on its own.

Before he left London Dunmore had joined Miller, Bonnamy and

Company, of which John Miller from West Florida was the chief partner. It was through Miller that Dunmore became associated with William Augustus Bowles, a Maryland loyalist who, among other adventures during the Revolution, had been elected a war chief by the Creek Indians in the fighting around Mobile. Bowles, however, was overshadowed among the Creeks by another white chief, Alexander MacGillivray, a bitter rival. MacGillivray's empire depended upon his bargaining the support of his Indian allies in defending Florida against encroaching Americans in return for trading concessions from the Spanish authorities. His trading partners were William Panton and Robert Leslie, Scottish loyalists from Georgia who had fled to Florida and remained behind when other refugees went on to the Bahamas.

With MacGillivray's assistance, Panton and Leslie won Spanish favor and gained a monopoly on the Indian trade with stores at Mobile, Pensacola, and Apalachee, near St. Mark's. Although they were British nationals, Panton and Leslie were serving Spanish rather than British interests. The Bowles-Dunmore-Miller plan was to take over this trading empire for themselves and by converting or defeating MacGillivray, extend British influence over the Indians of the Southwest. Other British were doing the same in the Northwest, where Great Britain as yet refused to abandon Detroit and other border forts to the United States.

Dunmore and Bowles sent two expeditions against Florida. In October 1788, a small force landed near Fort George, but failing to attract the Creeks in sufficient number, found the Spanish there and at St. Mark's too strong to attack. Most of the group ultimately surrendered. Bowles returned to Nassau and, over the next two years, traveled to Canada and Great Britain to win Gov. Carleton's and William Pitt's support of the plan to establish British hegemony from Florida to Detroit.

Bowles found encouragement in London because of the current confrontation between Britain and Spain over the latter's seizure of British ships in Nootka Sound near modern Vancouver, British Columbia. But when Spain's retreat eased the threat of war, Pitt avoided an outright commitment except to recognize the Creeks as a sovereign nation, allowing Bowles to sail ships under their flag into the free port at New Providence.

Returning to Florida in December 1791, Bowles demanded similar trade concessions from the Spanish and, when they refused, seized

Panton and Leslie's store at Apalachee in January 1792. Then, tricked by an offer to negotiate, he foolishly went to New Orleans, where the Spanish imprisoned him. MacGillivray's death shortly afterward encouraged Dunmore and Miller to continue pursuing their plan with other agents until the Creeks murdered the agents. The ships they sent to open trade with the Indians in Florida were captured before they landed.

From that time on Dunmore fell deeper into trouble. Quite possibly his problems were not unconnected, for some of his political opponents in the Bahamas may have been associated with Panton and Leslie. Pressure for a new election intensified as the seventh year of the legislature elected in 1785 approached. So did the clamor for an audit of the public accounts. In 1791 Dunmore had to prorogue the assembly without enactment of the annual revenue bill because the legislature insisted upon linking it with the appointment of commissioners of accounts. But the next year, with war with France imminent, the treasury was too low to risk repeating the tactic. Dunmore was forced to sign a bill limiting the life of a legislature to seven years, although for the moment he took refuge in a clause suspending the statute until the Privy Council in England signified its approval.

The voting on these issues in 1792 was close. Alternately the assembly would defy the governor and uphold him in the same session, as when it seated Philip Dumaresq in a disputed election in which Dunmore had interfered. Three days later it demanded again to see the receiver general's accounts. The session of 1793 went more smoothly, perhaps in anticipation of the ministry's verdict on the septennial act, or possibly because Dunmore had obtained a General Court opinion that British revenue acts automatically applied if the local legislature failed to enact one.

But in 1794 the Privy Council's ratification arrived, and Dunmore was at last compelled to hold the long-awaited election. When his supporters lost the majority, the governor met the situation by proroguing the assembly until the fall of 1795. At that time, he attempted to compromise by offering excerpts from the financial records. The assembly responded, however, by petitioning for Dumaresq's removal from office, forcing Dunmore to dismiss them until the next spring. By then, he had capitulated, probably because he had also lost support in Great Britain. He appointed James Menzies, his personal secretary of many years, to replace Dumaresq

as receiver general, and the latter, ill and confronted with imprison-
ment for contempt of the legislature, finally turned over his records
which the assembly referred to the British Privy Council.

By votes of twelve to eight and eleven to nine, the lower house
called for extensive constitutional reform. It passed resolutions
demanding more frequent elections, proper auditing procedures,
extension of representation to additional islands, and an increase in
the size of the Council. It also censured the governor for his frequent
prorogations of the legislature, his interference in assembly elections,
his sheltering of Dumaresq, and his "disrespect." But on a final
petition for his recall, the motion failed nine to ten. Three days later
Dunmore called the representatives to the Council Chamber, signed
the bills presented, and said, "It is with no little satisfaction that I find
myself now enabled, by the termination of Public Business, to put an
end to this session."

In Great Britain the complaints against Dunmore could not have
arrived at a worse time for him. A year and a half before, to
strengthen his government in the face of the French Revolutionary
War, William Pitt had brought into the cabinet the duke of Portland
and others of the faction that had been out of power since the defeat
of Fox's India bill, resulting in the resignation of Dunmore's patron,
the former Earl Gower, now marquis of Stafford. About the same
time the story exploded in the newspapers that Dunmore's daughter,
Augusta, who had remained in Great Britain with her mother when
he went to the Bahamas, had secretly married Prince Augustus
Frederick, a younger son of George III, without the king's consent in
violation of the Royal Marriage Act. The king was so angry that the
marchioness of Stafford had to apologize to him for finding herself in
the same room with Augusta when she once visited Lady Dunmore,
her sister, as she lay ill.

Most infuriating to the king was the fact that, although it was
unlikely they would inherit the British throne, any male heirs of
Augustus Frederick would stand high in the line of succession as
rulers of Hanover. German law, unlike British, prohibited females
from succeeding to a throne, and there was a dearth of males among
George III's grandchildren. The scandal dragged on twelve years
before the affair was settled with an annulment and the bestowal of a
title and handsome pension on Augusta and her children.

Dunmore no longer had protection against his enemies. In July
1796 he was dismissed as governor and ordered home immediately to

give an account. "Immediately" to him meant the next spring. Neither Pitt nor Portland would give him the satisfaction of more than a cursory interview, and the Treasury held up payment of about a quarter of the bills for the forts. But in the end the money was paid, and Dunmore was allowed a pension of £600. Considering the king's rage and the political pit into which he had fallen, Dunmore escaped amazingly well. He and Lady Dunmore retired to a well-known seacoast resort, Ramsgate in Kent, in the southeast of England, where he died on February 25, 1809.

BIBLIOGRAPHY

THE most detailed and authoritative study of Dunmore's American career is Percy B. Caley's doctoral dissertation at the University of Pittsburgh in 1939, "Dunmore: Colonial Governor of New York and Virginia, 1770–1782," which has not been published. Caley cut through the myths that grew around Dunmore in Virginia historiography without excusing him; Virginia's last royal governor had enough faults without inventing any. The six boxes of Dunmore Papers in the Earl Gregg Swem Library of the College of William and Mary, Williamsburg, Virginia, became available after Caley wrote. These are family manuscripts from the late seventeenth to the nineteenth century, and for purposes of this study are richest on Dunmore's military and political career in the 1750s and 1760s. They supplement the Murray family history in G. E. Cohayne, comp., *The Complete Peerage of England, Scotland, Ireland, Great Britain, and the United Kingdom*, IV, Vicary Gibbs, ed., 542–544; XII, pt. 1, Geoffrey H. White, ed., 200 (London, 1916, 1953) as does Jane Carson, "Lady Dunmore in Virginia" (unpublished research report, Colonial Williamsburg Foundation Library, Williamsburg, Va., n.d.). Dunmore's property is listed in his loyalist petition, July 9, 1784, in A. O. 12/54, pp. 118–135, Public Record Office, available on microfilm from the Colonial Records Project, Alderman Library, University of Virginia, Charlottesville. There also is the "Report by John Burrell relative to the Earl of Dunmore's Coalworks," January 1769, in the Scottish Record Office, Edinburgh, and Helen J. Campbell, "Porto Bello, Bruton Parish, York County, Virginia," *Virginia Magazine of History and Biography*, LXIX (1961), 460–468. The countryside around the family seat in Scotland is described in William Nimmo, *A General History of Stirlingshire* (Edinburgh, 1777). For political background in Great Britain bearing on Dunmore's career, see: John M. Norris, *Shelburne and Reform* (London, 1963), 7–9; John Steven Watson, *The Reign of George III, 1760–1815*, Oxford History of England, 12 (Oxford, 1960), esp. 135n; *Dictionary of National Biography*, s.v. Leveson-Gower, Granville, first Marquis of Stafford; Bernard Donoughue, *British Politics and the American Revolution: The Path to War, 1773–1775* (N.Y., 1964).

77

Dunmore's view, and that of his fellow British, of the American resistance is found in the Original Correspondence—Secretary of State, 1774–1777, C.O. 5/1353, P.R.O. The efforts of Gen. Gage, Adm. Graves, Gen. Howe, and the Admiralty to assist Dunmore may be followed in Adm. 1/485 and 486, C.O. 5/92, 121, and 122, and W.O. 46/9, f.121, and 55/369, ff. 164–165, P.R.O. All are available through the Colonial Records Project. There is also Dunmore material in Clarence E. Carter, ed., *The Correspondence of General Thomas Gage, 1763–1775* (New Haven, 1931), and "The Aspinwall Papers," Massachusetts Historical Society, *Collections*, 4th series, X (Boston, 1871). Capt. Andrew Snape Hamond's diaries, 1775–1777, are in the Alderman Library. A gossipy account of events is in the correspondence of James Parker of Norfolk and Charles Steuart of Scotland. The papers are in the Liverpool Library and the National Library of Scotland, Edinburgh, respectively, and must be correlated to be read intelligently. Colonial Williamsburg Foundation Library has microfilm copies.

Material on Dunmore's War in the Draper Collection at the Wisconsin Historical Society is in Reuben G. Thwaites and Louise P. Kellogg, eds., *Documentary History of Dunmore's War, 1774* (Madison, Wis., 1905). Virgil A. Lewis, *History of the Battle of Point Pleasant* (Charleston, W. Va., 1909) is a brief account. John Connolly's narrative is in *Pennsylvania Magazine of History and Biography*, XII (1888), 310–324, 407–420; XIII (1889–1890), 61–70, 153–167, 281–291.

David J. May's *Edmund Pendleton, 1723–1803: A Biography* (Cambridge, Mass., 1952) contains the best, recent account of Virginia from 1774 to 1776, although confined to events in which Pendleton participated. A storehouse of information on Virginia in these years is Julian P. Boyd's copious annotation in the first volume of *The Papers of Thomas Jefferson* (Princeton, N.J., 1950). Also valuable are the first volumes of William Hutchinson and William M. E. Rachal, ed., *The Papers of James Madison* (Chicago, 1962), and Robert A. Rutland, ed., *The Papers of George Mason* (Chapel Hill, N.C., 1970). Other printed collections bearing on Dunmore's activities are: David J. Mays, ed., *The Letters and Papers of Edmund Pendleton*, I, Virginia Historical Society Documents, 8 (Charlottesville, Va., 1967), which contains letters of Gen. William Woodford; James C. Ballagh, ed., *The Letters of Richard Henry Lee*, I (New York, 1911, reprinted 1970); Worthington C. Ford, ed., *Letters of William Lee*, I (Brooklyn, N.Y., 1891); "The [Gen. Charles] Lee Papers," New-York Historical Society, *Collections* (1871–1872); Charles Campbell, ed., *The Bland Papers* (Petersburg, Va., 1840); and William Wirt Henry, *Patrick Henry: Life, Correspondence, and Speeches*, I (Richmond, Va., 1891, reprinted 1969).

Full runs are extant for the three *Virginia Gazettes* published in Williamsburg during this period by Alexander Purdie, John Dixon and William Hunter, and Clementine Rind, who was succeeded by her assistant, John

Pinckney. All are on microfilm with an index compiled by Lester J. Cappon and Stella F. Duff (Williamsburg, Va., 1950). John Hunter's *Virginia Gazette* (Norfolk) is also in microfilm. The two known issues of Dunmore's *Virginia Gazette* are in C.O. 5/1353, f. 323, P.R.O., available through the Colonial Record Project, and the Virginia Historical Society, Richmond. An excerpt from a third is in Peter Force, comp., *American Archives*, 4th series (Washington, D.C., 1837–1853), IV, 540. The exchange of pamphlets by John Randolph and Robert Carter Nicholas is in Earl Gregg Swem, ed., *Considerations on the Present State of Virginia, attributed to John Randolph, Attorney General; and Considerations on the Present State of Virginia Examined, by Robert Carter Nicholas* (N.Y., 1919). Dunmore's proclamation of November 7, 1775, is reproduced in Francis L. Berkeley, *Dunmore's Proclamation of Emancipation* (Charlottesville, Va., 1941). Benjamin Quarles, "Lord Dunmore as Liberator," *William and Mary Quarterly*, 3rd series, XV (1958), 494–507, presents an opposing interpretation to mine. Such records as exist of the first two Virginia conventions as well as related material are in William J. Van Schreeven, comp., and Robert L. Scribner, ed., *Revolutionary Virginia. The Road to Independence: A Documentary Record*, I–II, (Charlottesville, Va., 1973, 1974). The proceedings of the remaining three conventions and of the General Assembly of 1775 are in Force, comp., *American Archives*, 4th ser., II, 1185–1242; III, 365–430; IV, 75–148; and VI, 1509–1616. The "Journal and Reports of the Commissioners Appointed by the Act of 1777 to Ascertain the Losses occasioned to individuals by the burning of Norfolk and Portsmouth in the Year 1776," is printed with the *Journal of the House of Delegates* (Richmond, 1835), Document 43. The original testimony taken by the commissioners is in the Virginia State Library, Richmond, Auditors' Item 177.

The records for Dunmore's career after leaving Virginia are more scattered. The most important are: Edward H. Tatum, Jr., ed., *The American Journal of Ambrose Serle, Secretary to Lord Howe, 1776–1778* (San Marino, Cal., 1940), 80, 86, 126, 135, 138; John Fortescue, ed., *The Correspondence of King George the Third from 1750 to December 1783* (London, 1927–1938), III, 515; A. Aspinwall, ed., *The Later Correspondence of George III* (Cambridge, 1962), I, nos. 78, 545; *American Manuscripts in the Royal Institution of Great Britain*, Historical Manuscripts Commission, *Fifteenth Report* (London, 1904–1909), I, 92; II, 338, 438, 452–453; III, 179; *Manuscripts in Various Collections*, Historical Manuscripts Commission, *Fifteenth Report* (London, 1901–1913), VI, 177, 179; *Manuscripts of the Marquis of Lansdowne*, Historical Manuscript Commission, *Fifth Report*, Appendix (London, 1876), 236, 251. Dunmore material in the Public Record Office available in the Colonial Record Project is: A.O. 12/99, ff. 19, 22, 105, 112, 146, 151, 223, 227, 260, 270, 271, 302, 325; A.O. 12/100, ff. 39, 114, 204, 238, 332; A.O. 12/101, f. 224; A.O. 12/106, ff. 6, 7, 25, 27, 42; A.O. 12/54, f. 234; C.O. 5/175, pp. 521–524,

527–531, 533–535, 541–542, 545–547, 549–563, 565–568; T. 1/566, ff. 281–282; T. 1/580, ff. 112–119; W.O. 47/98, pp. 969, 1021; W.O. 47/100, pp. 121, 156. Mary Beth Norton, *The British Americans: The Loyalist Exiles in England, 1774–1789* (Boston, 1972) describes Dunmore as a lobbyist.

For Dunmore's career in the Bahamas, the principal source is the *Bahama Gazette* (Nassau), available on microfilm for 1784 to 1786 and 1789–1800. Dunmore's view of his dismissal is in the Colonial Record Project: P.R.O. 30/8/131. Michael Craton, *A History of the Bahamas* (London, 1962), chapters XV and XVI, tells the general story. Focusing on Dunmore's plans to regain the Southwest for Great Britain are: J. Leitch Wright, Jr., "Lord Dunmore's Loyalist Asylum in the Floridas," *Florida Historical Quarterly*, 49 (1970–1971), 370–379, and his *Anglo-Spanish Rivalry in North America* (Athens, Ga., 1971), 142–149, as well as Lawrence Kinnaird, "The Significance of William Augustus Bowles' Seizure of Panton's Apalachee Store in 1792," *The Florida Historical Society Quarterly*, IX (1931), 156–192. Background is provided by Charles L. Mowat, *East Florida as a British Province, 1763–1784*, University of California Publications in History, Volume 32 (Berkeley, Cal., 1943), 146–147; Francis Armytage, *The Free Port System in the British West Indies* (London, 1953), 104, 141; and Wilbur H. Siebert, "The Legacy of the American Revolution to the British West Indies and Bahamas," *The Ohio State University Bulletin*, XVII (1913), 6–50. Lady Augusta Murray's romance may be traced in Aspinwall, ed., *The Later Correspondence of George III*, II, nos. 1009, 1010, 1012, 1017, 1024, and A. Aspinwall, ed., *Correspondence of George, Prince of Wales, 1770–1812* (London, 1971), nos. 1022, 1480, 1482, 1488, 1490, 1506, 1509, 1600n, 1643, 1644, 1671, 1682, 1809, 2171n, 2299n, 2322n.